Praise for *Building Your House of Harmony*

"Raising children can be stressful, sometimes even maddening. Thus, parents need help—lots of it! Thankfully, we have the wise mind and warm heart of Deborah Winters. Based on science and decades of helping families flourish, Winters shares with us her blueprint for creating homes oozing with perspective, communication, and nurturance. A perfect blend of anecdotes, research, and practical advice, *Building Your House of Harmony* should be on every parent's nightstand and every teacher's desk."

— Jeffrey J. Froh, PsyD, author of *Thrive: 10 Commandments for 20-Somethings to Live the Best-Life-Possible*, and founder and past clinical director of the Positive Psychology Institute for Emerging Adults at Hofstra University

"I was excited but skeptical about this book. I've tried so many ways to get my teenage daughter to listen that I doubted there was anything new to learn. But the PCN Method wasn't about finding the perfect tactic; it was about shifting my own responses. Instead of trying to control hers, it helped me learn to connect with her, which has yielded so much more. Every parent wants to raise a good human, but this book helped me see that my job isn't to *make* one—it's to create an environment where they *become* one. With less pressure and more tools to create calm, I can now respond more effectively. A great book that empowers rather than shames parents."

— Rachel Joffe, LCSW and owner of Bricks and Minifigs, West Babylon

"While we unfortunately are not handed an owner's manual when we become a parent, Winters offers us a framework for parenting success that is both remarkably flexible and pleasantly intuitive. Guided by modern neuroscience research from scholars such as Dan Seigel, Winters's Perspective, Communication, Nurture (PCN) Method gives us step by-step tools to put space between our immediate, emotional reactions and a more intentional, nurturing, and grounded reaction to any tough parenting situation. The book reads as if Winters is there with you—guiding and coaching you with helpful ways to shift your perspective (e.g., from *He is being defiant* to *He is struggling with something*), allowing for increased connection and empathy. The PCN model is an exquisite guide for building attunement and communication in any relationship, and should be a definitive resource for anyone looking to survive and thrive in the child-rearing years!"

— Diana Milillo, PhD, LMHC, social psychologist, licensed mental health counselor, and certified clinical trauma professional

"This book will help countless parents struggling with daily conflicts with their children. Deborah's PCN Method offers a well-researched and actionable guide to create a nurturing and cooperative household by fostering understanding, using collaborative communication and reinforcing boundaries with love. The result is a connected, emotionally intelligent family capable of growth and adaptation. The PCN Method also helps children develop resilience, self-discipline, and problem-solving skills that they can take with them into the world. Deborah's approach is universally applicable and generationally healing."

— Karin Sabbeth, LCSW-R, relational, psychodynamic and attachment-based therapy specialist

"Deborah Winters's *Building Your House of Harmony* offers a ground-breaking approach to parenting that goes far beyond traditional advice, providing a comprehensive framework for understanding and connecting with children through her innovative PCN (Perspective, Communication, Nurture) Method. By integrating neuroscience research with practical strategies, Deborah gives parents a transformative road map for developing emotional intelligence and resilience in their children. The book's unique strength lies in its ability to guide parents through self-reflection while offering actionable tools that can be applied across different developmental stages. Deborah convincingly demonstrates how small shifts in parental perspective and communication can create profound, lasting changes in family dynamics. This is an essential guide for any parent seeking to build deeper, more meaningful relationships with their children."

— Janice V. Johnson Dowd, LMSW therapist, speaker and author of *Rebuilding Relationships in Recovery: How to Connect with Family and Close Friends After Active Alcoholism and Addiction*

"I am a very permissive parent; some would even call me a pushover. Deborah's PCN Method taught me how to set boundaries my children listen to—so that I can be a leader my kids listen to, connect with, and respect. Thanks to *Building Your House of Harmony* I now know how to guide my children toward the behavior I want to see while providing them with a loving environment in which they feel supported, safe, and confident enough to be themselves. A win-win!"

— Joanne Kountourakis, owner and editor of the *Northport Journal*

"As someone deeply involved in supporting families, I recognize the critical need for parents to have robust tools to navigate today's complex challenges. The PCN Method provides a comprehensive approach to understanding children's needs, building resilience, and establishing boundaries that can prevent serious behavioral issues. Drawing from clinical expertise, Deborah offers an easy-to-follow, transformative framework for fostering emotional well-being and creating a supportive environment where children can truly thrive. A must-read for parents seeking to build stronger, more compassionate family relationships."

— Linda Oristano, executive director of AWARE Drug & Alcohol Community Coalition

"Raising kids in today's digital world comes with unique challenges, and the PCN Method has been a game changer for me. The perspective piece is huge. It's helped me step back, see situations through my kids' eyes, and respond with more patience and understanding instead of frustration. I carry it with me everywhere, using its insights to navigate tough moments and to create stronger connections with my kids. This framework has given me the confidence to guide my children with clarity and purpose. I rely on the PCN Method daily."

—Krystle Schultz, social media and marketing consultant and founder of M2 Marketing and Social Media and the Learn to Earn course

Building
YOUR HOUSE
OF HARMONY™

A Parent's Blueprint tc Cooperation,
Respect, and Lasting Change

DEBORAH WINTERS, LCSW
CLINICAL THERAPIST AND PARENT COACH

MEDIA.COM

The views and opinions expressed in this book are those of the author and do not necessarily reflect the official policy or position of Illumify Media Global.

Published by
Illumify Media Global
www.IllumifyMedia.com
"Let's bring your book to life!"

Paperback ISBN: 978-1-964251-58-5

Cover design by Debbie Lewis

Printed in the United States of America

Dedications

To my daughters Kayla and Brynn,
You are my greatest teachers. Every day, you remind me why this work matters. This book is for you—so you always know the power of feeling seen and understood.

To my husband, Craig,
Through every challenge, late night, and moment of doubt, you stood beside me—not just holding things together but holding *me* together. This book exists because of your quiet strength, endless encouragement, and the space you gave me to grow.

To my friends and family members,
Your love and support have been my foundation. Thank you for always cheering me on.

Contents

Introduction

Did you ever imagine parenting would feel this hard? Perhaps you lie awake at night replaying the day's arguments, wondering how conversations that started with simple requests ended in slammed doors and tears. Maybe you've tried everything—reward charts, punishments, counting to three, positive affirmations—yet still find yourself trapped in cycles of conflict that leave both you and your child/teen feeling more disconnected than ever.

Over the past decade as a clinical therapist, I have had the privilege of working with countless families, listening to their struggles, hopes, and fears. Through these conversations, one fundamental truth has consistently emerged: at the core of nearly every family conflict lies a deep, often unspoken need to feel genuinely understood—not just heard, but truly seen and validated for who they are and what they are experiencing.

Picture this: Your child comes home, slams their backpack down, and snaps at their sibling. Your immediate instinct, born from love and concern, is to jump in with solutions: "Take a deep breath," "Use your words," or "Go to your room until you can behave." But in that rush to fix the problem, something crucial gets lost—the opportunity to understand what's really happening in your child's world.

There is often a gap between feeling loved and feeling understood, creating a disconnect that fuels most family struggles. Your children know you love them—that's never been the question. But somewhere between your deep desire to protect them and your natural instinct to fix their problems, they lose the sense that you truly understand their experience. When children don't feel understood, they either push back harder or withdraw completely, leaving parents feeling helpless and wondering where they went wrong.

Think about your own childhood for a moment. What memories resonate the most? Was it the punishments, the lectures, the quick fixes? Or was it those rare, precious moments when someone took the time to really understand what you were feeling? When you felt truly seen, not just corrected?

As both a therapist and a mother of two, I've witnessed firsthand how our best intentions to help our children can actually create more distance. We rush to solve problems before our children feel understood. We offer solutions before they feel heard. We enforce consequences before they feel safe enough to share what's really bothering them. And with each quick fix, the gap between us grows wider.

I am here to teach you another way.

What if I told you that the key to transforming family conflict isn't about finding better punishments or more creative rewards? What if the path to cooperation isn't through control but through connection? And what if that connection begins not with making your child understand you but with you understanding them?

The PCN communication method I developed—which stands for Perspective, Communication, and Nurture—emerged from years of watching families transform when they learned to prioritize understanding before action. This isn't another variation of "gentle parenting" that leaves you feeling powerless, nor is it a rigid system of control that damages your relationship. Instead, it's a practical framework built on three fundamental human needs that every child (and adult) requires for healthy development and attachment:

1. The need for connection, fulfilled through understanding and logical **Perspective**
2. The need for self-determination, achieved through **Communication**, with Choices or Collaboration
3. The need for safety, established through consistent limits and boundaries with **Nurture**

When these three elements work together, something remarkable happens. Arguments decrease not because children become more compliant but because they feel more understood. Cooperation increases not from fear of consequences but from a new sense of self-discipline. Most importantly, children begin to feel safe enough to share their struggles, trust their parents' guidance without resistance, and learn from mistakes without fear of judgment.

If you're exhausted from the daily battles, worried about the growing distance between you and your child, or simply seeking a more effective way to discipline, you're in the right place. Whether your child is a toddler testing boundaries or a teenager pushing for independence, the PCN Method provides a blueprint for building what I call your House of Harmony—a home where understanding flows both ways, where mistakes become opportunities for growth, and where connection powers cooperation.

Through these pages, you'll discover

◈ Ways to see beyond behaviors to understand the deeper needs driving them

- ◈ Approaches to create genuine connection before attempting correction
- ◈ Methods to set boundaries that strengthen rather than strain relationships
- ◈ Techniques to guide without controlling
- ◈ Strategies to build lasting cooperation through understanding
- ◈ Tools to help your children develop emotional intelligence and self-discipline
- ◈ Steps to transform your home from a battlefield into a sanctuary of growth and learning

The journey to building your House of Harmony starts with a simple sentiment: your child isn't giving you a hard time—they're *having* a hard time (Greene 1998). When you learn to truly understand before trying to be understood, to connect before correcting, and to nurture through consistent, caring boundaries, you create the conditions for lasting positive change.

The peace you're seeking isn't about perfect behavior or unwavering compliance. It's about creating a home where every family member feels safe, understood, and capable of growth. A home where love isn't just felt but truly understood. Welcome to your House of Harmony.

1

The Evolution of Parenting

"Do the best you can until you know better. Then when you know better, do better."

—Maya Angelou

Sarah stared at her reflection in the bathroom mirror, trying to steady her breathing as tears threatened to spill over. Just ten minutes ago, she'd lost her cool—again—over what should have been a simple morning routine.

"Mom, I told you I can't find my blue shirt!" Jake had yelled from upstairs. "The one I 'need' for the presentation!"

She'd reminded him three times last night to get his clothes ready. She'd even offered to help, but he'd insisted he'd handle it. Now here they were, twenty minutes before they needed to leave, and the morning was already derailing.

"It's in the laundry basket on your bed," she called back, making lunches for Jake and his sister, Emma, while simultaneously signing her daughter's permission slip. "I folded it yesterday."

"No it's not! I already looked there!"

Sarah closed her eyes, counted to three—just like all the parenting books suggested—and climbed the stairs to help. But when she walked into Jake's room to find the laundry basket dumped on the floor, clothes scattered everywhere, her carefully crafted patience crumbled.

The blue shirt was right there, half-buried under his comforter.

That's when it happened. All the frustration from countless mornings like this one, all the exhaustion from trying to keep everyone on track while working full-time, all the guilt from feeling like she should be handling it better—it all came pouring out.

"I can't believe you made this mess when the shirt was right here!" she snapped. "How many times do we have to go through this? You're eleven years old, Jake! You need to be more responsible!"

His face crumpled, and Emma appeared in the doorway, wide-eyed at the commotion. In that moment, Sarah saw herself through their eyes—red-faced, angry, a far cry from the patient, understanding mother she'd always sworn she would be.

Now, locked in the bathroom, Sarah wondered how she'd gotten here. She'd read all the books, followed all the different "parenting" social media accounts, tried all the recommended techniques. She was doing everything "right"—or at least everything the experts said was right. So why did every morning still feel like a battle? Why did simple requests turn into power struggles? Why did she still find herself yelling, despite promising herself each night that tomorrow would be different?

Sarah splashed cold water on her face and took a deep breath. She had to get back out there, had to salvage this morning somehow and get everyone to school. But deep down, she knew something had to change. She couldn't keep cycling through calm mornings that devolved into chaos, couldn't keep attempting the same strategies that clearly weren't working.

If you've ever found yourself in a similar moment—locked in a bathroom, hiding in your car, or just staring at the ceiling at night wondering where you went wrong—you're not alone. Like Sarah, you might be doing everything the parenting books suggest, yet still finding yourself trapped in cycles of nagging, yelling, and conflict. You might also be wondering why the techniques that worked when your kids were younger don't seem to work anymore or why, despite your best efforts, simple requests often spiral into full-blown battles.

The truth is, it's not your fault. And more importantly, it's not too late to change.

Remember the early days of parenthood?

Your tool kit was deceptively simple: a warm bottle, a favorite lullaby, a gentle touch. Like a well-rehearsed dance, you knew exactly which moves would soothe your crying infant or coax that precious baby to smile. Those first years felt manageable because the solutions were clear-cut. Hungry? Feed them. Tired? Rock them to sleep. Upset? Hold them close.

But as your children grow, so does the complexity of their needs. That trusty old tool kit—the one that worked like magic during the diaper years—now feels inadequate for modern parenting challenges. Your children are developing their own thoughts, opinions, and, most challenging of all, their own digital lives. Those "because I said so" moments that once smoothed over any argument now meet with raised eyebrows and reasoned rebuttals.

Think of it like trying to repair a smartphone with a hammer and screwdriver. The tools aren't bad; they're just not designed for today's challenges. Modern parenting requires a more sophisticated approach: tools for digital-age guidance, emotional intelligence, and maintaining connection while setting boundaries. What parents need now is a new tool kit designed for contemporary challenges—one that helps navigate social media, information overload, and the complex balance of achievement and well-being.

The good news? Just as you mastered those early parenting skills, you can learn and adapt to these new challenges too. The key lies not in longing for the simplicity of the past but in developing new techniques that honor both your children's growing independence and your evolving role in their lives.

Where Are You Now?

Before we dive deeper, let's take a moment to reflect on your current parenting experience. Find a quiet space, grab a journal or open the notes app on your phone, and consider these questions:

- How would you describe your day-to-day experience with your children?
- When was the last time you felt truly confident in your parent-child communication?
- What specific behaviors or situations leave you feeling overwhelmed?
- How often do you find yourself yelling or implementing consequences that don't seem to work?
- When did parenting start feeling harder, and what changed?

These reflections aren't just exercises—they're important markers on your parenting journey. You'll revisit these questions as you develop new tools, so keep your answers somewhere safe. They'll serve as a powerful reminder of how far you've come.

Why Modern Parenting Feels Harder

If you're feeling overwhelmed by modern parenting, you're not alone. The challenges parents face today are vastly different from those of previous generations, making traditional parenting approaches feel inadequate. From managing the digital landscape to keeping up with the new modern childhood, parenting has become increasingly complex. Below I explain five of the most significant challenges reshaping the parenting landscape.

The Digital Revolution

Your child's world is dominated by technology that didn't exist in your childhood. Beyond basic screen time management, you're navigating social media pressures, online safety, and digital communication norms that transform how children learn and interact. Your child likely develops digital literacy skills faster than you can keep up, requiring constant adaptation to new platforms while trying to set healthy boundaries. When your child prefers texting to talking, traditional parenting approaches need significant adjustment.

Shifting Social Dynamics

The supportive village that previous generations relied on has largely disappeared. Geographic distance from family, weakened community connections, and demanding work schedules leave you navigating complex decisions in isolation. Social media amplifies this challenge by creating unprecedented pressure to be the "perfect" parent. Each decision feels scrutinized, while carefully curated online parenting moments, highlighting in others' social media reels, can make normal struggles feel like personal failures.

Information Overload

Every parenting decision now comes with endless, often conflicting advice. Social media influencers, parenting experts, and online communities bombard you with opposing viewpoints about the "right" way to parent. This constant stream of information can leave you doubting your instincts and hesitating when quick decisions are needed. A simple question about sleep training can spiral into hours of research with no clear answers.

Modern Child Development Research

New understanding of child development adds complexity to your parenting decisions. Research shows that emotional intelligence rivals academic achievement in importance, and children's brains develop primarily through relationships and experiences. This knowledge challenges traditional discipline approaches and educational choices, requiring you to question methods that worked for previous generations.

Achievement Pressure

Your child faces earlier academic expectations and more structured activities than ever before. The pressure to excel starts in preschool, while the definition of success grows increasingly complex. You're constantly balancing enrichment opportunities with protecting your child's emotional well-being and preserving their childhood experience.

The Natural Evolution of Parent-Child Relationships

In addition to the modern-day challenges presented above, there is a natural evolution that both parents and children go through as children age. Understanding how parent-child relationships naturally evolve is crucial for updating your parenting tool kit. When your trusted methods suddenly stop working, it's easy to feel like you're failing. But these moments often signal that your child has entered a new developmental stage—one that requires different tools and approaches.

In *The Whole-Brain Child*, drawing from their influential work on child development, authors Dr. Daniel Siegel and Tina Payne Bryson (2011) highlight the critical importance of parental adaptability. A parent's ability to grow and adjust their approach based on a child's changing needs can serve as a fundamental predictor of positive outcomes. Understanding these developmental stages helps explain why your old parenting tools might no longer be effective. The following sections will clarify these stages and help you anticipate the changes you are noticing and adapt your approaches with confidence to match your child's developing needs.

Foundation Years (Pre-Birth and Early Infancy)

During this foundational period, parents are building their initial tool kit through research, preparation, and imagination. "I won't be 'that' kind of parent," or "I will do things differently than my parents did."

Then your baby is born, and you learn to read your baby's cues and master the basics of care. While you might have entered parenthood with detailed plans, your baby quickly teaches you to adapt to their unique needs.

Authority Builder (Toddler/Preschool)

Your little one discovers the word *no* and tests every boundary. That simple infant care tool kit of bottle and lullabies evolves as you balance nurturing with limit-setting. You're learning the delicate dance of encouraging independence while maintaining necessary structure.

World Interpreter (School-Age)

Your role expands to helping your child understand an increasingly complex world. Beyond basic care and discipline, you're now supporting homework, navigating friendships, and handling bigger emotions. Your tool kit grows to include deeper conversations and more nuanced guidance.

Growing Independence (Preteen)

The parent-child dynamic shifts dramatically. Your direct authority gives way to more collaborative approaches as your child develops stronger opinions and peer relationships. Success now means learning to guide and influence rather control and make decisions for them.

Negotiation Master (Teen Years)

Welcome to the delicate balance of freedom versus safety. Your teenager requires room to grow while still needing your guidance. Your tool kit must expand to include strong communication skills, emotional regulation, and the ability to choose your battles wisely.

Trusted Advisor (Late Teens/Early College)

Your role transforms from manager to consultant. Rather than directing, you're now supporting independence while remaining a trusted resource. It's time to master the art of offering guidance without overstepping.

Adult Connection (Young Adult Years)

Your relationship evolves toward adult friendship. Your tool kit focuses on maintaining meaningful connection while fully respecting your child's independence. You're learning to celebrate achievements from a supportive distance.

Embracing Change as Self-Care

It's completely natural to feel overwhelmed as you navigate the ever-changing landscape of parenting. In fact, research suggests that as you adjust to your child's evolving needs, your brain is actively forming new neural pathways. This process can feel awkward at first, much like trying to write with your non-dominant hand. The encouraging news is that with consistent effort, new habits can become second nature in about two months (Lally et al. 2009).

Embracing these changes isn't just about becoming a better parent—it's a profound form of self-care. When you acknowledge that your parenting needs to evolve and take steps to develop new tools, you're not just helping your child; you're modeling resilience, adaptability, and emotional intelligence. You're showing them that growth, even when it's uncomfortable, is valuable and achievable. Self-care at its best!

Think of updating your parenting tool kit to build your House of Harmony as a form of professional development for the most important job you'll ever have. Just as a skilled craftsperson continually learns new techniques and acquires better tools, effective parents recognize that their methods must evolve as their children grow. It's a mark of wisdom and commitment to your family's growth.

 Remember: The discomfort you feel when old methods stop working isn't a reflection of your parenting abilities. It's simply a signal that it's time to expand your tool kit. Just as your child is growing into new capabilities and understanding, you, too, are growing into a more sophisticated, nuanced version of yourself. This evolution, while challenging, is exactly what successful parenting looks like in the modern age.

Signs You're Ready for New Tools

You might recognize some of these indicators that it's time for a tool kit upgrade:

- Your go-to responses aren't getting the results they used to.
- You find yourself repeating the same phrases with diminishing effect.
- Your child seems more resistant to your traditional approaches.
- You feel stuck in cycles of conflict despite your best efforts.
- Your relationship feels more strained despite trying harder.
- You're exhausted from parenting and miss the easier days.

These signs don't mean you're failing—they mean you're ready for the next phase of your parenting journey. Your new parenting tool kit!

Remember Sarah from our opening story? Let's peek in on her six months later.

It's another weekday morning, and Jake can't find his basketball jersey for the afternoon game. But this time, the scene plays out differently.

"Mom?" His voice carries down the stairs, tinged with worry but not panic. "I can't find my jersey. I've looked in my drawer and the laundry basket."

Sarah feels that familiar flutter of anxiety—they're on a schedule, after all—but instead of rushing upstairs with a frustrated sigh, she pauses. "Okay, when did you wear it last?" she calls back, keeping her voice calm and curious.

"Tuesday's practice." There's a moment of silence, then, "Oh! I left it in my gym bag!"

Sarah smiles, recognizing a moment that once would have spiraled into tears and accusations now resolving itself with just a little space for thinking. She hears the zip of his gym bag, followed by a triumphant "Found it!"

This isn't a story about perfect parenting—Sarah still has her moments, and Jake still occasionally leaves his homework until the last minute. Emma still sometimes pushes back against bedtime, and mornings don't always run smoothly. But something fundamental has shifted.

The tools Sarah discovered in her parenting evolution—the same ones you'll learn about in the coming chapters—haven't just changed how she parents; they've transformed how she sees her role in her children's lives. Where she once felt responsible for managing every detail, preventing every mistake, and solving every problem, she now understands that her job is to guide, support, and coach her children toward their own solutions.

The nagging has been replaced by curiosity, the yelling by connection, and the conflict by collaboration. It's not because her children suddenly became perfect or because she discovered some magical parenting secret. It's because she learned to update her parenting tool kit using the PCN Method for the family she has now, not the family she had three years ago.

As you stand at the beginning of your own journey toward creating your House of Harmony, you might be feeling like Sarah did that morning in the bathroom—overwhelmed, defeated, and wondering if change is really possible. Take heart in knowing that every parent who has successfully navigated this evolution started exactly where you are now.

In the next chapter, you'll dive deep into the PCN Method, your new parenting toolbox, giving you practical tools to begin your own transformation. But for now, take a moment to acknowledge the courage it takes to recognize when change is needed. Feeling overwhelmed isn't a sign of defeat—it's often the first step toward meaningful growth. Your willingness to explore new approaches, question old patterns, and imagine a different way of parenting is already setting the foundation for the transformation ahead.

As you close this chapter, consider returning to those reflection questions you explored earlier. Your answers will serve as a baseline, a "before" picture of sorts, as you begin implementing the tools and strategies in the coming chapters. And perhaps, six months from now, you'll have your own "jersey morning" story to tell—a moment when you realize that what once would have triggered chaos instead flows with connection and calm.

Welcome to the next phase of your parenting journey. Let's begin building your House of Harmony together.

2

Introducing Your New Parenting Tool Kit to Building Your House of Harmony

"Behind every young child who believes in himself is a parent who believed first."

—Matthew Jacobson

L isa gripped her steering wheel, letting out a long exhale as she sat in the school pickup line. The email from ten-year-old Ben's teacher still burned in her mind: "Ben continues to be disruptive during class reading time." She'd tried everything—reward charts, consequences, taking away screen time—but nothing seemed to stick. Just this morning, she'd caught herself cycling through her usual script:

"Ben, how many times do I have to tell you . . ."

"If you don't listen, then . . ."

"Why can't you just . . ."

Each phrase felt like another brick in the wall growing between them. The more Lisa "tried," the more it felt Ben was pushing back harder. The sweet little boy who used to curl up in her lap for story time now rolled his eyes and slammed doors. The afternoon battles over homework, the constant reminders to read, the explosive arguments over screen time—it all left her feeling like she was failing at the one job she wanted to get right.

Last night had been the breaking point. After yet another argument about finishing reading before video games, Ben had looked at her with tears in his eyes and shouted, "You never listen to me! You don't understand anything!"

Those words hit harder than any door slam. Because deep down, Lisa knew he was right. She'd been so focused on getting Ben to listen to her that she'd stopped listening to him. All her parenting tools seemed to center around getting compliance, but something was missing. There had to be a better way to reach her son, to rebuild the connection they'd lost somewhere between kindergarten and fifth grade.

As the pickup line inched forward, Lisa noticed the parenting book she'd tossed onto the passenger seat that morning. Its promise of a "House of Harmony" had seemed almost too good to be true when she'd ordered it. But right now, standing in the ruins of her own parenting confidence, she was ready to try something different. Anything different.

If you've ever felt like Lisa—exhausted from the daily battles, worried about the growing distance between you and your child, and desperate for a new approach—you're in the right place. What if instead of trying to use the same exhausted tools from your existing parenting tool kit, it's time to build something entirely new?

Can you picture this house?

You're standing before an empty lot, blueprints in hand, ready to build not just any house but your dream home—a sanctuary where every beam and brick serves a purpose, where every room flows seamlessly into the next, and where harmony reigns supreme. This is precisely the journey you're embarking on—except you're not building a physical house. You're constructing something far more precious: your House of Harmony, a framework for creating lasting peace and connection in your family through the PCN Method.

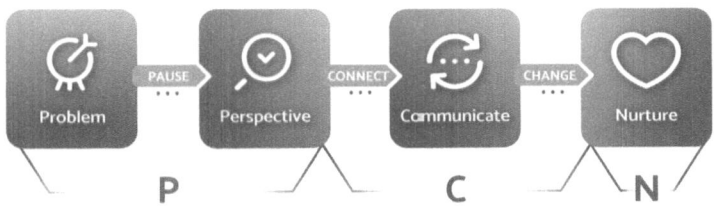

Understanding the PCN Method

The *P* stands for Perspective – how you view and understand your child's behavior.

The *C* stands for Communication – how you engage with your child to solve problems.

The *N* stands for Nurture – how you support and encourage positive changes for the long haul.

These three tools work together to meet three essential human needs:

- ◈ Connection
- ◈ Self-determination
- ◈ Safety

The **P** Stands for Perspective: A Powerful Tool for Building Genuine Connection

Ever wonder why some conversations with your kids feel like you're talking to a brick wall, while others create those magical moments of real connection? It all comes down to something scientists call "perspective taking," and it's simpler than you might think.

Picture this: your child is having a meltdown over something that seems tiny to you—like wearing the "wrong" color socks. Your instinctive reaction is to dismiss or shame their feelings by telling yourself something like, *I don't understand why this is so difficult!* or *It's like he purposely wants to make me late!* Instead, you try to see the world through their eyes by considering something like, *I wonder why these socks didn't bother him yesterday but are today,* or *Is there something else going on other than the socks?*

The idea is to use this new perspective to then connect with your child. That would sound like, "It seems like these socks are really bothering you; that has to be so frustrating!" or "Is it really the socks, or do you need a little extra cuddle time this morning?"

When a parent approaches a situation from a different perspective, something remarkable happens in the brain.

For a parent, they feel calmer, more in control. For the child, they feel heard, understood, and ready for change. When children feel understood, their emotional state can shift from one of distress, or "fight, flight or freeze," to a calmer, more receptive state, as supported by Dr. Daniel Siegel and Tina Payne Bryson's (2011) research on emotional regulation and brain development.

Think of it like tuning a radio: When you find the right frequency (their perspective), the static clears up, and suddenly you're both on the same channel. Not only does your child feel more secure, but they become more open to working through challenges together.

Perspective helps you to

◈   see beyond challenging behaviors to understand their true causes

◈   recognize your own emotional triggers and responses

◈   align your expectations with your child's developmental stage

◈   build deeper connection through understanding

This connection isn't just feel-good parenting; it's science-backed relationship building that creates the foundation for positive change. Now you're ready to move into the *C* mode.

 Remember: Taking your child's perspective doesn't mean giving in to demands or accepting inappropriate behavior. Instead, it's the essential first step in your parenting tool kit— creating the connection needed for effective communication and positive change. When children feel understood, they become more receptive to guidance and boundaries.

The C Stands for Communication: Honoring the Need for Self-Determination

Imagine Chris's frustration when he asked his fifteen-year-old, Joey, to clean his room, only to hear: "I was going to, but now I don't want to because you told me to." Sound familiar? That pushback might feel like defiance, but there's actually something deeper happening.

All humans have a fundamental need for autonomy—to feel like they have some control over their lives. When Joey resisted, he wasn't just being difficult; he was expressing this basic human need for self-determination. It's the same feeling adults get when someone tells them to do something they were already planning to do—suddenly, the natural motivation disappears.

How parents support this need for autonomy looks different depending on their child's age. And teaching children how to achieve this self-determination in appropriate ways is crucial for their own interpersonal relationships in life.

For older kids like Joey, it means bringing them into the problem-solving process as active participants through collaboration.

But for younger children, like Joey's four-year-old brother, Max, it might look more like offering simple choices: "Would you like to put away your blocks first or your trucks?"

Using his perspective about one's need for control and autonomy, Chris turned this once power struggle with his son into a teaching moment. Instead of escalating the situation, he took a breath and tried a different approach: "You know what? I hear you saying you want to handle this your own way. I get it, as I like being in charge of my own choices too. Your room needs to be cleaned before you can go out with your friends later. What time will you get it done?" This simple shift in perspective transformed their interaction. Joey went from defensive to engaged, explaining he had already planned to clean his room after finishing his homework.

Chris acknowledged his son's autonomy while still maintaining appropriate boundaries: "I love that plan. As long as it's done before going out, you can choose when."

Here's what made the difference:

- ◈ Chris recognized Joey's pushback as a healthy sign of developing independence.
- ◈ He created space for his son to voice his own plans instead of forcing compliance.

◈ They found a solution that respected the need of both parent and child for autonomy and the household's needs.

◈ The focus shifted from control to collaboration.

By seeing beyond the initial resistance, Chris also helped Joey learn how to assert his independence constructively—a skill that will serve him well throughout life. It's not about letting kids do whatever they want; it's about helping them develop healthy self-determination while understanding the balance between independence and responsibility.

 This shift in approach isn't always easy, especially in those triggering moments of apparent defiance. But remember, when children push back, they're often just practicing their emerging sense of autonomy. Our job as parents isn't to break that spirit but to help shape it into something powerful and positive—whether that means collaborative problem-solving with our teens or offering appropriate choices to our toddlers. When children feel they have a voice in decisions that affect them, their motivation for positive behavior soars.

The **N** Stands for Nurture: Addressing the Fundamental Need for Safety

Maria and her sixteen-year-old daughter, Sophia, are sitting at the kitchen table, having what could have been a heated argument about curfew. Instead, they're actually talking. "I know you want me home by 10:00, Mom," Sophia says, "but the movie ends at 9:45, and it takes at least twenty minutes to get home. Could we make it 10:30?"

When parents maintain clear, consistent boundaries while remaining open to reasonable negotiation, children develop a deeper sense of security. This safety allows them to explore independence while knowing exactly where the lines are drawn. Maria and Sophia worked out a compromise: a 10:30 curfew, with Sophia agreeing to text when the movie ends and again when she's heading home.

The real test came the following weekend. Sophia's texts came as planned, but 10:30 came and went: 10:45 . . . 11:00 . . . When Sophia finally walked in at 11:30, she launched into a string of excuses about traffic and losing track of time.

Here's where the true nurturing happened—not in permissiveness or control, but in following through. Maria remained calm: "I hear your reasons, and I believe you didn't intend to be late. But we had an agreement. As we discussed, this means you'll need to skip next weekend's movie night."

Despite Sophia's protests, Maria held firm. This wasn't punishment for punishment's sake—it was about creating predictable patterns that help children develop better decision-making skills. When parents respond consistently to boundary crossings, children learn to better anticipate outcomes and adjust their behavior accordingly.

The next weekend, Sophia was frustrated about missing the movie, but something interesting happened. She started planning better, leaving more buffer time for traffic. These natural consequences helped her develop better judgment and impulse control.

This kind of nurturing helps to

- build trust through predictable responses
- model boundary setting and reliability by following through
- create space for learning from mistakes
- demonstrate that rules exist for their safety, not control

Real nurturing isn't always soft and cuddly. Sometimes it's standing firm on boundaries while saying, "I love you too much to let this slide. I know you can learn from this." When consequences are consistent and proportional, children develop stronger emotional regulation skills and better decision-making abilities.

This is how lasting change takes root—through consistent, loving boundaries that show your children you believe in their ability to grow and learn, even when (especially when) they stumble along the way. The balance of nurture and structure helps children develop both emotional awareness and rational thinking skills, building the foundation for lifelong success.

Think the curfew example seems strict? As a reminder, it is there to illustrate the key principle: clear boundaries with consistent follow-through help children feel secure and learn responsibility. Later chapters will explore how to collaborate with your child to establish age-appropriate limits and natural consequences that work for your family.

The PCN Method: Building Long-Term Success Through Essential Human Needs

When the PCN Method addresses these three foundational human needs—connection through **Perspective**, self-determination through **Communication**, and safety through **Nurture**—children develop more than just "better" behavior; they gain essential life skills. Like your child moving from meltdown to understanding over mismatched socks, or like Joey discovering independence through collaborative problem-solving, or like Sophia learning time management through consistent boundaries.

As children experience this balanced approach—being understood, having appropriate control, and feeling secure within loving limits—they develop the internal resources needed for lifelong success. The result isn't just peaceful moments at home; it's about children being equipped with the emotional intelligence, decision-making skills, and relationship wisdom to thrive throughout their lives.

Building Your House of Harmony Using the PCN Method

Like any skilled builder knows, it's not just about having the right tools; it's about knowing when and how to use them. When you learn to use the tools of the PCN Method effectively, something remarkable happens. It doesn't just help you build a better home; it helps you become a more confident, regulated parent with clearer communication, better boundaries, and less guilt and anxiety.

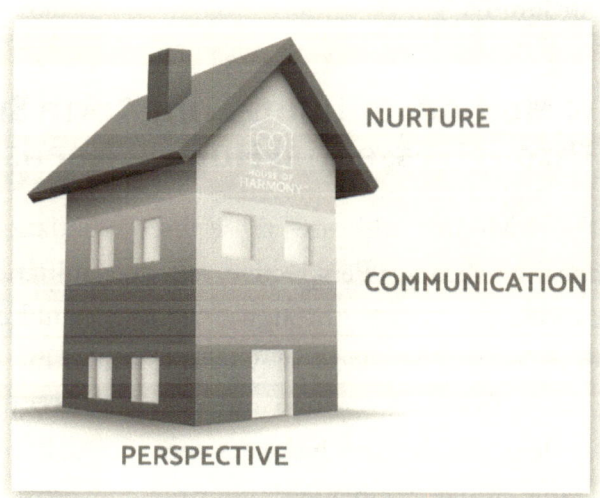

Let's look at how the three components of the PCN Method work together to build your House of Harmony.

It begins with **Perspective** as the foundation—taking the time to understand your child's viewpoint creates the stable ground of connection that everything else will build upon. Without this foundation, like any poorly grounded structure, your parenting efforts may crack under pressure.

Next, you will raise the walls through **Communication**, generating strong, age-appropriate ways of creating changes to behavior while allowing for openness and flow, much like the beams of your home provide both structure and living space. When you communicate in ways that honor self-determination, you create rooms where everyone feels heard and valued.

Finally, you'll top your house with the protective roof of **Nurture**, sheltering and preserving the harmony you've built below. This nurturing cover provides the safety essential for your family to weather any storm, while protecting the warm, secure environment you've created within.

When your perspective lens is clear, your communication strong, and your nurturing consistent, you're not just building a house; you're creating a legacy of emotional intelligence, healthy boundaries, and family connection that will stand the test of time.

Your Blueprint for Success

As described, the PCN Method isn't just another set of parenting techniques—it's a comprehensive tool kit for building lasting family harmony. In the upcoming chapters, you'll explore in detail how each component of the PCN Method works together to build your House of Harmony.

Just as Rome wasn't built in a day, your House of Harmony will need to develop over time. Each small step, each implemented strategy, each moment of connection adds another brick to your family's foundation of trust and respect. The PCN Method provides the blueprint—your commitment and consistency will bring it to life.

Where is Lisa now? you might be wondering.

Six months after learning the PCN Method, Lisa's journey with her son Ben shows how these tools work together to create lasting change. When Ben's teacher reported his disruptive classroom behavior, Lisa's first step wasn't to punish or lecture—instead, she put on a logical lens in the **Perspective** phase. Through careful observation and calm conversations, she discovered Jake felt anxious and restless during long periods of sitting, and his disruptions were actually attempts to self-regulate.

With this understanding as her foundation, Lisa moved to the **Communication** phase, working collaboratively with Ben to brainstorm solutions. Together, they came up with several strategies: a silent stress ball he could squeeze when feeling fidgety, scheduled movement breaks between subjects, and a subtle signal he could use to let the teacher know he needed a quick walk to the water fountain. All of which his teacher happily supported.

The real power of the PCN Method showed in the **Nurture** phase. Both Lisa and Ben's teacher maintained consistent follow-through with both rewards and consequences they'd agreed upon during their collaboration. When Ben used his new strategies successfully, he earned extra outdoor time. On days when he forgot and fell back into disruptive behaviors, he spent part of his free time practicing his classroom coping skills, like taking a short physical break to walk to the water fountain and reset his focus.

Today, Ben's teacher reports a dramatic improvement. And Lisa notes, "Instead of feeling frustrated and helpless, I now have tools that help me understand, connect with, and guide my son."

But the real success isn't just in Ben's better behavior—it's in the skills he's developed. Through perspective, he gained self-awareness about his own needs. Through communication, he learned to solve problems for himself in collaboration with others. And through nurture, he experienced how consistent boundaries could help him grow.

Like the House of Harmony itself, these changes aren't just temporary fixes—they're a foundation Ben can build on for years to come. Their House of Harmony wasn't perfect—what real home is? It was just a home where both mom and son felt heard, understood, and valued.

As you move forward, you'll explore each component of the PCN Method in detail. Remember that you're not just learning new techniques; you're building a new home for your family's relationships to grow and thrive. Every small shift in perspective, every thoughtful conversation, every nurturing response adds another brick to your foundation.

Let's start building.

3

Perspective – The Foundation to Your House of Harmony

"When you change the way you look at things, the things you look at change."

—Wayne Dyer

Picture the strongest house you've ever seen. What makes it unshakeable isn't the paint color or the window trim—it's the foundation beneath it all. In your House of Harmony, that foundation is perspective, and its strength determines everything you'll build above it.

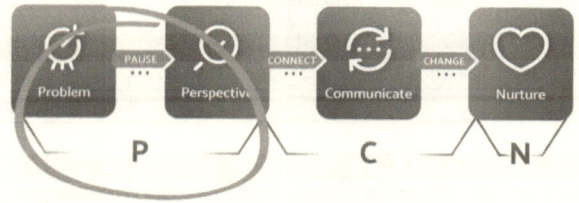

What You Focus On Is What You Feel

Jenny stared at her phone, scrolling through the text messages of yet another argument with her fifteen-year-old daughter, Layla. Late homework assignments, forgotten chores, attitude problems—her mind raced through a growing list of concerns. Each notification brought a fresh wave of frustration and worry. *Why can't she just be more responsible?* Jenny thought, feeling her anxiety rise.

Then she remembered something from her parenting workshop: "What you focus on is what you feel"—a concept that supports Dr. Aaron Beck's (1963) pioneering ideas on cognitive behavioral therapy that our thoughts influence our emotions, which then shapes our actions.

Taking a deep breath, Jenny started scrolling back further through their messages. There, between the tense exchanges, she found different stories: Layla helping her younger brother with his science project without being asked, a thoughtful good morning text with a heart emoji, a picture of them laughing together at last week's family dinner.

That evening, instead of starting with "Did you finish your homework?" Jenny opened with, "I was thinking about how you helped Marco with his project last week. That was really kind of you." Layla, braced for another lecture, softened visibly. For the first time in weeks, they had a real conversation.

Later, Jenny reflected on how shifting her focus had transformed not just her feelings but their entire interaction. The challenges hadn't disappeared—there was still homework to discuss and chores to complete—but by choosing to focus first on Layla's strengths, she'd created space for connection. And in that space, solutions seemed more possible.

Sometimes the biggest changes in family harmony don't come from fixing problems but from adjusting the lens through which you view them.

The Science of Perspective: Understanding Your Parent Brain

Your brain is masterfully designed for survival. Neuroscience research reveals that your amygdala—the brain's alarm system—processes potential threats in milliseconds, far faster than the rational mind can engage. This lightning-quick response system, essential for human survival, doesn't distinguish between physical dangers and emotional triggers.

Dr. Daniel Siegel and Tina Payne Bryson's (2011) research on brain development demonstrates that when parents perceive a child's behavior as threatening—even just emotionally—the brain reacts the same way it would to a physical threat: by activating the fight-flight-freeze response. This is why something like a toddler's tantrum or a teenager's eye roll can feel so intense.

But here's where the power of perspective comes in. While you can't control that initial, survival-based thought, cognitive behavioral research shows you absolutely can control what happens next.

Dr. Beck's (1963) work on how thoughts influence emotions and behaviors shows us exactly where that power lies—and it's right between your ears. The image below illustrates how your thoughts shape your feelings, which in turn shape your actions.

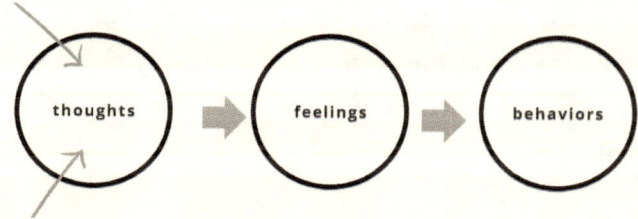

Most parents get caught in an emotional cascade: they feel frustrated, angry, or hurt, and react from that emotional space without ever examining the thoughts that created those feelings.

Think of it this way: your brain's initial reaction is like an overprotective security guard. While the guard means well, it often mistakes typical childhood behavior for a serious threat. When you let that first reactive thought drive your response, it can derail effective parenting. But when you pause and check the story your brain is telling you, you gain the power to respond more calmly and intentionally.

The Choice Point: From Reaction to Response

While you may not have control over that first thought, you always have control over the second thought!

Picture your first parental reaction like an overprotective alarm system—quick to sound at any hint of trouble. While this instant response served our ancestors well, it's not always helpful in modern parenting. The good news? You have the power to pause between that first thought and your response.

When parenting from that first reactive thought, you often view typical childhood behaviors as defiance, seeing daily challenges as threats rather than opportunities for growth. These quick reactions tend to be emotional rather than thoughtful, causing you to miss valuable moments for teaching and connection with your child. In these reactive moments, the focus shifts to correction rather than under-standing, creating a cycle of frustration for both you and your child.

But there's a moment—a choice point—between your first thought and your response. In this pause, you can shift from reaction to intention. This simple practice of pausing to consider a second, more balanced thought changes not just your response but the entire interaction with your child.

Instead of thinking, *He's being defiant again*, you might think, *He's struggling with something*.

Rather than *She never listens*, you might consider, *She needs a different approach*.

This shift in perspective opens up new possibilities for connection and teaching, transforming challenging moments into opportunities for growth—both yours and your child's.

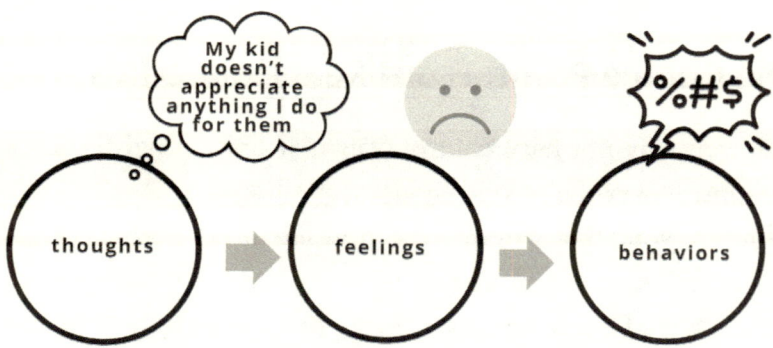

What you think is what you feel, and what you feel is what you do. If you're thinking your kid is ungrateful, lazy, or unappreciative, you're most likely going to feel discouraged, angry, or frustrated. This in turn may cause you to react emotionally.

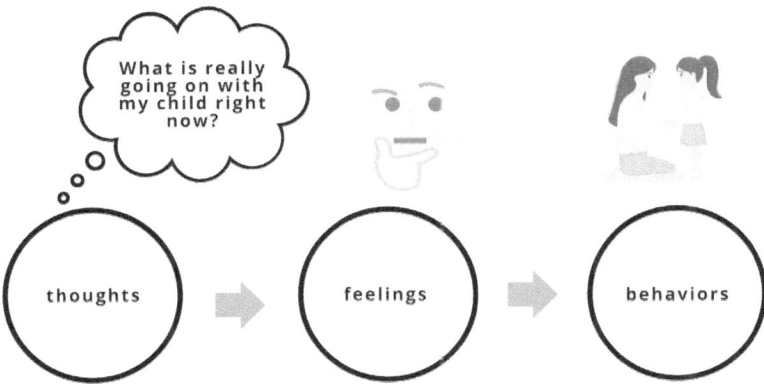

The more logically a parent is *thinking*, the better they will *feel*, which then leads to a parent responding to a hard situation more meaningfully and more in line with what is truly happening. Not what the parent thinks is happening. This results in more ideal outcomes that create real changes to unpleasant behaviors.

Building Connection Through Perspective

The true power of perspective lies in its ability to create connection—a fundamental human need. When you learn to pause between your first thought and your response, you make room for understanding rather than reaction. Instead of defaulting to *She's manipulating me* or *He's pushing my buttons*, you can shift to *She's having a hard time* or *He needs help with big feelings*.

This shift isn't just about feeling better—it creates real change in how you and your child interact. When you approach challenging behaviors with curiosity instead of judgment, you're better equipped to empathize and problem-solve together. By building your foundation on perspective, you're not just changing how you see your child's behavior; you're transforming how you respond to it.

This is why perspective forms the bedrock to your House of Harmony. Without it, even the best parenting strategies crumble under pressure. With it, you create a foundation strong enough to maintain family connection, even during life's stormiest moments.

Exercise 1: Looking Through the Storm

Think about a recent challenging moment with your child—one that still stirs up emotions when you recall it. Maybe your teenager slammed their door during an argument about screen time, or your toddler had a meltdown in the grocery store.

Take a moment to write about what happened:

Now, dive deeper into the emotional impact:

- ◈ What thoughts ran through your mind in that moment?
- ◈ How did those thoughts make you feel about yourself as a parent?
- ◈ How did they make you feel about your child?
- ◈ What actions did these feelings lead to?

What happened after? (Check all that apply)

- ❑ I raised my voice.
- ❑ I said things I regretted.
- ❑ I gave a punishment I later questioned.
- ❑ I withdrew or shut down.
- ❑ I spent hours replaying the situation.
- ❑ Other: _____

Exercise 2: Shifting the Lens

Now, let's reimagine that same situation, but through a different lens. Perhaps a homework battle, screen time argument, or bedtime struggle. Now imagine approaching that same situation from a different perspective. What if, instead of immediately reacting, you paused to understand?

Picture how the interaction might shift when you lead with curiosity rather than correction. Your voice stays steady, your shoulders relax, and you create space for your child to feel heard. While boundaries remain firm, they're delivered with understanding rather than frustration. Even in disagreement, you maintain connection. This different lens doesn't mean giving in—it means approaching challenges from a place of understanding first, then moving forward together to find solutions.

Reflect on this new perspective:

4. What feels different in your body when you imagine this version?
5. What new possibilities open up in your imagination when you approach the situation this way?
6. How does this shift change how you se
   ◈ yourself as a parent?
   ◈ your child?
   ◈ the situation itself?

The Power of Your Perspective

Look back at both scenarios and notice the striking differences in how each situation unfolded. In your first reaction, the words that likely came to mind—*frustrated, overwhelmed, helpless*—may have led to responses you later regretted. But when viewing the same situation through a different lens, words like *understanding*, *patient*, and *connected* emerged, creating very different outcomes.

This dramatic shift came from one thing: changing your perspective. The challenging situation didn't change—your lens did. This is the foundation of the PCN Method. When you shift your perspective, you transform emotional reactions into logical responses. This opens new possibilities for connection and gives you access to more effective parenting tools. Most importantly, it creates space for teaching and growth in moments that might otherwise spiral into conflict.

Remember: This exercise isn't suggesting that parenting challenges will magically disappear. Instead, it demonstrates how your perspective acts as the foundation for everything that follows. When you build your response on understanding rather than reaction, you create space for the connection and growth that define your House of Harmony.

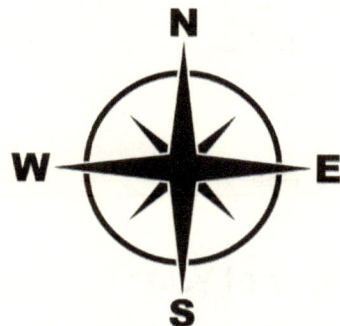

THE RIGHT PERSPECTIVE ACTS AS
YOUR PARENTING COMPASS

4

Understanding Your Child's Behavior Can Impact Your Perspective

"When your child feels truly safe, doors swing open to positive change."

—Dr. Karyn Purvis

A s parents, when you see beyond surface behaviors to understand their deeper meaning, your entire approach to parenting begins to shift. The more you understand about your child, the clearer your perspective. The clearer your perspective, the less likely you are to make hasty judgments based solely on immediate actions.

Meaning, rather than reacting to the tantrum, defiance, or withdrawal, you begin to recognize each of these as a signal. A meltdown over homework might reveal anxiety about falling behind. A teenager's sharp words could mask fears about fitting in. A child's refusal to try new things might stem from worry about failure.

Research consistently shows that behavior serves a purpose or communicates a need, a principle supported by the work of Webster-Stratton and Reid (2004). This understanding changes how you handle challenging moments. When you can see what's really going on behind behaviors, you can lead conversations with more empathy, addressing what's driving the behavior rather than just trying to stop it. When you recognize that children do well when they can, struggles become opportunities to teach missing skills rather than just correct misbehavior. This approach then leads to better solutions and less conflict.

Perspective Shifts in Action: Old vs. New Understanding

Scenario 1: Homework Resistance

◈ Old perspective: *She's lazy and unmotivated. She just wants to play on her phone instead of doing her work.*

◈ New understanding: *She seems to struggle most with getting started on complex assignments. This might be showing me that she needs help breaking down big tasks into manageable steps,* or *I wonder if she needs to learn how to set better limits with her phone. It seems to be distracting her.*

Scenario 2: Morning Meltdowns

◈ Old perspective: *He's just being difficult and trying to make us late. He needs to learn responsibility.*

◈ New understanding: *He has trouble with transitions, especially in the morning when he's tired*, or *I wonder if there is something going on at school that is causing him to meltdown like this.*

Scenario 3: Social Withdrawal

◈ Old perspective: *She's being so shy. Why does she act like this? It's so embarrassing and rude.*
◈ New understanding: *Maybe she's a little more introverted and needs time to warm up*, or *I wonder if school drains her energy. Perhaps she needs a little time to recharge and balance her social energy.*

Scenario 4: Aggressive Play

◈ Old perspective: *He's a menace and needs to learn to control himself. This behavior is unacceptable.*
◈ New understanding: *Why is he unable to stop himself from unsafe situations? We've talked about this. I wonder if there is something more going on that I need to speak to a professional about*, or *Does he have the vocabulary to express his feelings? How can I teach him to speak to me when he's feeling overwhelmed?*

Scenario 5: Bedtime Battles

◈ Old perspective: *She can be so manipulative and controlling. She just wants to get her way.*
◈ New understanding: *Her heightened anxiety at bedtime might indicate separation concerns or a need for more connection during the day*, or *I wonder if she is sleeping badly and needs help developing better routines and habits.*

The Ripple Effect of Understanding

When you shift from quick judgment to deeper understanding, a remarkable transformation occurs in your parenting. Your responses become more measured and thoughtful, allowing your child to feel truly seen and validated. This validation creates a foundation of trust where solutions emerge more naturally. Instead of power struggles, you find teaching moments. Rather than focusing solely on correcting behavior, you build deeper connection. This understanding allows for meaningful growth—not just behavioral changes but real emotional development. This leads to the real changes you want that grow with your family for a lifetime.

As you continue reading, you'll discover more about what drives both your child's behavior and your own reactions, giving you additional tools to strengthen this foundation of understanding. Again, your perspective becomes more than just a viewpoint—it develops into a deeper awareness that transforms your entire parenting approach.

Shifting Perspective: Understanding the Causes of Your Child's Behaviors

Have you ever wondered why your child behaves so differently than their siblings, or why strategies that work perfectly for one family seem to fail in yours? The truth is your child's behavior is shaped by an intricate dance between nature and nurture—a complex interplay of factors as unique as their fingerprint. By understanding these influences, you gain more than just knowledge; you gain the power to respond with empathy, set effective boundaries, and guide your child's development with confidence.

Ten Core Factors That Shape Behavior

1. *Innate Characteristics.* Each child arrives with a unique temperament that influences how they navigate the world. Some children naturally buzz with energy, while others move at a calmer pace. Sleep patterns vary dramatically—one child might sleep soundly through any noise, while another wakes at the slightest sound. Social preferences also differ, with some children eagerly seeking company, while others need quiet time to recharge. While genetics contribute to these traits, your child's environment plays an equally important role in shaping how these characteristics develop.

2. *Birth Order.* Your child's position in the family uniquely influences their development. Only children often excel in adult interactions but may need extra support with peer relationships. Firstborns typically emerge as natural leaders, though they might struggle when attention shifts to siblings. Middle children often become skilled negotiators and peacekeepers, while youngest children frequently develop strong social skills but might need extra encouragement toward independence.

3. *Developmental Stages.* From birth through adolescence, children progress through distinct developmental phases. While all children develop at different speeds, knowing the basics for each stage will allow for a more accurate interpretation of a child's abilities.

   Babies (0–18 months): During the first 18 months, your baby's development centers on building fundamental trust and exploring their world. A newborn learns that crying brings comfort—when hungry, you feed them; when wet, you change them. By six months, they discover cause and effect through daily play: dropping toys to watch them fall or learning that shaking a rattle creates sound.

Your presence becomes increasingly important as attachment grows—notice how your baby might cry when you leave the room but light up when you return. Everything is a sensory experience at this age: they put toys in their mouth to understand texture, grab at faces to explore features, and study everything intently as they build their understanding of the world. This foundation of trust and exploration shapes how confidently they'll venture into toddlerhood.

Toddlers (18–36 months): Welcome to the "me do it!" phase. Your toddler now asserts independence in every way possible insisting on putting on their own shoes (even if it takes ten minutes), choosing their own clothes (stripes with polka dots), and climbing into the car seat themselves.

Language explodes during this period, moving from single words to short phrases. "Mine" becomes a favorite word as they grasp ownership, leading to playground negotiations over toys. Boundaries are tested constantly: they'll look right at you while reaching for the forbidden remote, not from defiance but from learning where the limits are. While this phase can test your patience, it represents crucial steps toward independence.

Preschoolers (3–5 years): Welcome to the world of "why" questions and elaborate pretend play. Your preschooler now crafts detailed stories, turning cardboard boxes into spaceships and creating invisible friends. Social skills develop through playground interactions as they learn to take turns, share, and navigate early friendships. They might tell you about the dragon in their room or insist their stuffed animals need dinner—this blending of reality and fantasy is normal as they sort out the difference between real and pretend. Big emotions still overwhelm at times (like full meltdowns over a broken crayon), but they're gradually learning to express feelings with words instead of just actions.

School Age (6–11 years): The school-age years bring a dramatic shift as your child's world expands beyond family. Friendships become increasingly complex, moving from simple playground buddies to deeper relationships with inside jokes and secret handshakes. Their thinking becomes more sophisticated—they can solve problems step by step and understand cause and effect beyond the immediate moment. You'll notice them wrestling with bigger concepts like fairness, questioning why different families have different rules. They begin forming their own identity through activities and interests, maybe declaring themselves a "soccer player" or "artist." This is when they start comparing themselves to peers and developing a stronger sense of who they are in relation to others.

Adolescents (12–18 years): Welcome to the roller coaster of adolescence. Your teen's drive for independence intensifies—they may spend more time in their room, question family rules, and prioritize friends over family time. Their body and brain undergo significant changes, affecting everything from sleep patterns (they're not being lazy; their biological clock actually shifts) to emotional responses. Social acceptance becomes crucial as they figure out where they fit in. Their thinking grows more sophisticated; they can debate complex topics and consider hypothetical scenarios. While they push for freedom, they still need your guidance—just delivered differently than before. Think of them as an apprentice adult, learning to balance independence with responsibility.

4. *Environmental and Social Influences.* Your child spends most of their waking hours in settings beyond home—school, activities, and social groups. These environments powerfully shape behavior. A child who's typically outgoing at home might become quiet in class, or a reserved child might become animated at sports practice. Peer influence grows stronger with age, especially during adolescence when acceptance becomes paramount. Your child learns unspoken social rules through these interactions: when to speak up in class, how to join a playground game, or what behaviors earn social approval.

5. *Media Impact.* Today's children navigate a world saturated with digital influences. Screen time affects more than just homework habits—it shapes attention spans, social skills, and expectations about relationships and success. A child watching peers' carefully curated social media posts might feel inadequate about their own life. Gaming can affect sleep patterns and real-world social interactions.

6. *Neurological and Mental Health.* The brain's wiring significantly influences behavior. A child with ADHD might struggle to sit still, not from defiance but because their brain processes attention differently. Anxiety might make a capable student hesitate to raise their hand in class. Learning differences can affect how a child approaches tasks—what looks like procrastination might actually be overwhelm.

7. *Physical Health and Wellness.* Basic physical needs dramatically impact behavior. A child refusing to cooperate might simply need sleep—just as adults get cranky when tired, children's emotions become harder to manage when exhausted. Hunger affects focus and patience. Exercise isn't just about physical health; it helps regulate emotions and improve concentration.

When facing behavioral challenges, always check these fundamental needs first.

8. *Trauma and Adversity*. Past difficult experiences shape current behavior. A child who experienced instability might hoard snacks or struggle with transitions. What appears as "attention seeking" might really be connection seeking. A child who experienced loss might resist getting close to others. Understanding trauma's impact helps parents respond with patience instead of punishment.

9. *Gender Roles*. Society sends messages about "appropriate" behavior for boys and girls from an early age. A boy might hide his interest in art because peers label it "girly," while a girl might downplay her love of science to fit in. Parents can help children navigate these expectations while staying true to their interests and abilities.

10. *Parenting Style*. Your parenting approach fundamentally shapes your child's behavior. Think of it as setting the emotional temperature of your home. Strict rules with little warmth can often produce anxious or rebellious behavior. Too few boundaries with unlimited warmth can leave children struggling to self-regulate. The sweet spot combines clear expectations with emotional support, helping children develop both self-discipline and self-confidence.

What Is My Child's Behavior Telling Me?

As Dr. Ross Greene famously said, "Kids do well if they can," highlighting the belief that children will succeed when provided with the appropriate support and skills (1998, 28).

Let's pause for a moment and let that sink in. How many times have you found yourself thinking, *Why are they doing this to me?* when your child is acting out? But here's the game-changing truth: your child's behavior is actually their way of communicating a need, and your emotional reaction is often the key to understanding what that need is.

Think of behavior like a smoke signal; it's trying to tell us something. And just like smoke signals, sometimes the message can get a bit cloudy. But here's the interesting part: how that behavior makes *you* feel is a huge *clue* about what your child is trying to communicate.

Let's break down the four main messages your kids might be sending through their behavior, a concept rooted in Dreikurs and Soltz's book *Children: The Challenge* (1964), which outlines the four goals of misbehavior: attention, power, revenge, and avoidance of failure.

1. "Notice Me!" (The Need for Attention)

Children may misbehave to seek attention if they feel they can't get it in positive ways. This behavior will most likely annoy the parent, leading the parent to correct the child's behavior through reminding, yelling, nagging, etc. Even negative attention can reinforce the behavior. This creates a cycle where the child continues to seek more attention.

How it feels to you: annoying, irritating, like you can't get anything done.

What it looks like in real life . . .

Picture this: You're on an important work call, and your eight-year-old, who was happily playing just moments ago, suddenly needs to show you every Pokémon card in their collection. You whisper, "Not now," but they get louder, dropping cards, making exaggerated movements. With each "Hang on" from you, their behavior gets more disruptive until you're forced to end your call early.

Sound familiar? That's classic attention-seeking behavior. Your annoyance is the clue—they've found a reliable way to get your attention, even if it's negative.

2. "I Need Some Control" (The Need for Power)

Some children seek power and control over their parents by misbehaving, refusing to follow instructions or throwing tantrums. When a child seeks power, the parent feels angry. If the parent fights the child, the child fights back. If the parent gives in, the child has won the power struggle and thus stop misbehaving.

How it feels to you: angry, challenged, like you're in a tug-of-war.

What it looks like in real life . . .

It's time to leave for school, and you ask your nine-year-old to put on their shoes. Simple request, right? But they move in slow motion, examining each shoelace like it's a fascinating science experiment. When you say, "Hurry up," they go even slower. Your blood pressure rises as you watch them deliberately tie and retie their shoes, silently communicating, *You can't make me do this any faster.*

The power struggle is real, and your rising frustration is the signal that your child is seeking control.

3. "I'm Hurt" (The Need for Understanding through Revenge)

Children who desire control but are unable to win power struggles with their parents may seek revenge to feel a sense of belonging. This could include saying or doing hurtful things or staring angrily at the parent, leading to a cycle of revenge between the child and parent. As a result, both parties end up with hurt and angry feelings.

How it feels to you: hurt, wounded, shocked by their behavior.

What it looks like in real life . . .

Your twelve-year-old has just been told they can't go to a friend's house until their room is cleaned. Instead of cleaning, they rip down the family photo you just hung on their wall, declaring, "I hate this family anyway!" Your heart drops—this feels like a personal attack, and that's exactly why they chose this behavior. They're hurting and want you to feel their pain.

When your child's behavior causes you emotional pain, they're often trying to communicate their own emotional pain.

4. "I Can't Do It" (The Need to Avoid Failure)

Children who feel unable to succeed may display feelings of inadequacy and give up, causing parents to feel hopeless and want to give up on the child. This tends to happen in one area of the child's life at a time, such as schoolwork, sports, or other social activities.

How it feels to you: helpless, frustrated, wanting to give up.

What it looks like in real life . . .

> Your eleven-year-old used to love soccer but now claims they're "sick" before every practice. When you encourage them to try, they respond with "I'm the worst player anyway" or "Nobody wants me on their team." Your heart sinks as you watch their confidence crumble, and you feel helpless to fix it.

That feeling of helplessness is your clue that your child is displaying feelings of inadequacy as a means to avoid failure.

A New Perspective Guide

Next time your child's behavior triggers a strong emotion in you, try this quick check-in:

1. Notice how you're feeling (annoyed? angry? hurt? helpless?).
2. Use that feeling as a clue to what your child might need.
3. Ask yourself, *What might my child be trying to tell me?*

For example,

◈ If you're feeling annoyed → They might need attention in a positive way.
◈ If you're feeling challenged → They might need some appropriate control.
◈ If you're feeling hurt → They might need emotional understanding.
◈ If you're feeling helpless → They might need encouragement and support.

Understanding Transforms Everything: A Review

In this chapter, you've discovered how behavior serves as your child's primary language of communication. You've learned that actions—from tantrums to withdrawal, from defiance to clingy behavior—carry deeper meanings. Through exploring the ten core factors that shape behavior, you now understand how temperament, birth order, development stages, environment, and other influences create your child's unique behavioral landscape.

This knowledge transforms frustrating moments into opportunities for connection. When your teenager slams their door, you can look beyond the action to see possible social anxiety. When your toddler melts down over a broken cookie, you recognize it might be about feeling powerless rather than being difficult.

Looking ahead, the next chapter explores another crucial piece of the puzzle: your own behavior patterns. You'll discover how your experiences, triggers, and automatic responses influence your parenting perspective. By understanding both your child's and your own behavioral drivers, you'll build an even stronger foundation for your House of Harmony.

QUICK GLANCE
FOUR GOALS OF BEHAVIOR

	ATTENTION	POWER/CONTROL	REVENGE	INADAQUACY
HOW DO YOU FEEL?	Bothered Annoyed	Angry Threatened	Hurt	Hopeless Like giving up
WHAT DO YOU DO NEXT?	Remind, nag, scold	Punish, fight back, or give in	Bothered Annoyed	Give up, agree that the child is helpless
HOW DOES YOUR CHILD RESPOND?	Stops temporarily. Later, misbehaves again	Continues to misbehave, defies you, or does what you've asked slowly or sloppily	Misbehaves even more, keeps trying to get even	Does not respond or improve

This chart is adapted from Dreikurs, R., & Soltz, V. (1964). *Children: The challenge*. Hawthorn Books.

5

Understanding Your Own Behavior Can Impact Your Perspective

"The only thing that is keeping you from getting what you want is the story you keep telling yourself."

—Tony Robbins

U nderstanding your child's behavior begins with understanding yourself. This chapter explores two powerful tools that enhance your parenting perspective: 1) Recognizing your emotional triggers and 2) Identifying your natural parenting style. Just as understanding your child's behavior creates connection, understanding your own patterns builds a stronger foundation for your House of Harmony.

Tool 1: Recognizing Your Emotional Triggers

Remember that morning when you promised yourself you wouldn't yell, wouldn't nag, wouldn't lose your cool? Then seven thirty rolled around, shoes couldn't be found, breakfast was refused, and despite your best intentions, you found yourself raising your voice—again.

You're not alone. Most parents don't wake up wanting to yell or feel disconnected from their kids. They don't plan to have power struggles or end their days feeling guilty about how they handled things. Yet it happens, and understanding why is the first step to changing it.

Think of your emotional regulation system like a cup of water. Every parent starts their day with a different amount of space in their cup, based on five key factors:

1. *Your Brain on Parenting.* As you learned in chapter 3, your brain has a built-in smoke detector, the amygdala, which serves as the brain's "alarm system," activating a fight-flight-or-freeze response when it perceives a threat. In parenting, stress can cause the amygdala to become overactive, making it harder to respond calmly to everyday challenges.

   Suddenly, you're reacting to spilled milk like it's an emergency. Your body floods with stress hormones, making you feel instantly angry over minor issues. You might snap at normal kid behaviors like slow breakfast eating or forgotten backpacks. This automatic stress response can trigger reactions before your logical brain has time to engage, leaving you with a shorter fuse than usual for typical childhood moments.

2. *The Hormone Dance.* Your body's chemical balance significantly influences your parenting reactions. Hormonal fluctuations—whether from postpartum changes, monthly cycles, or

age-related shifts—affect both men's and women's emotional responses. You might notice days when everything feels overwhelming or find yourself more emotional than usual. These natural chemical changes can amplify your reactions to normal parenting challenges, making some days feel particularly difficult to navigate with patience and calm.

3. *The Sleep Factor.* Think of your emotional regulation like a phone battery. When well rested, you operate at full capacity, but sleep deprivation—an all-too-familiar state for parents—drains your reserves quickly. Running on low sleep affects your ability to parent effectively, leaving you with less patience for typical challenges. You might struggle to find creative solutions to everyday problems and find yourself quicker to anger or tears. Just as you'd prioritize charging a depleted phone, recognizing sleep's impact on your parenting helps you understand why some days feel harder than others.

4. *The Stress Load.* Modern parenting carries a heavy weight of demands—work deadlines competing with soccer practice, financial pressures clashing with child care needs, relationship balancing acts, and the constant internal questioning about parenting decisions. These pressures accumulate invisibly until your capacity feels maxed out.

What might have been manageable on a good day—a child's repeated requests or a change in routine—suddenly feels like the last straw. Your reactions may intensify, snapping at minor infractions, feeling overwhelmed by typical morning chaos, struggling to juggle competing needs. This accumulated stress affects how you respond to everyday parenting challenges, making typically manageable situations feel insurmountable.

5. *Your Childhood Echo.* Your childhood experiences created a deep blueprint for handling emotions. Those early lessons—whether emotions were dismissed with "Stop crying!" or expressed through yelling—often resurface in your parenting moments. You might catch yourself using the exact phrases you swore you'd never say, or notice your reactions mirror your own parents' responses.

   Even when you consciously choose a different parenting path, these ingrained patterns can emerge during stressful moments. Recognizing these childhood echoes helps explain why certain situations trigger stronger reactions than others, and why changing these automatic responses requires both awareness and practice.

Transforming Triggers into Tools

Understanding your emotional triggers transforms them from parenting obstacles into opportunities for growth. When you recognize what drains your emotional cup—whether it's lack of sleep, work stress, or echoes from your own childhood—you can take action before reaching the empty point. These triggering moments become valuable signals rather than sources of shame.

Think of triggers as your personal parenting GPS. Just as your phone alerts you to traffic ahead, your triggers warn you when you need extra support or self-care. That flash of frustration over a messy room might signal you're overwhelmed in other areas of life. The quick anger at dawdling might mean you're running on empty and need to refill your own cup first.

This awareness creates a powerful choice point. Instead of automatically snapping when your child takes forever to put on shoes, you might notice your rising stress and take a deep breath first. Rather than yelling about a forgotten homework assignment, you could pause to consider if your reaction matches the situation.

By understanding your triggers, you're also breaking generational patterns. You're showing your children that emotions can be understood rather than just reacted to. Every time you catch yourself and choose a different response, you're laying new foundation blocks in your House of Harmony.

Tool 2: Understanding Your Parenting Style

Now that you've explored how your own triggers can impact parenting, let's look at another crucial piece of the perspective puzzle: your parenting style.

Think of your parenting style as your default operating system—the automatic way you respond in challenging moments. When your child refuses homework, talks back, has a meltdown in public, or tests boundaries, your true parenting patterns emerge, especially when stressed or tired.

Research on parenting styles, first identified by Diana Baumrind (1967) and later expanded by Maccoby and Martin (1983), shows that most parents naturally lean toward one of three main approaches: the Director (Authoritarian), the Friend (Permissive), or the Guider (Authoritative). Each style comes from a place of love and good intentions but leads to different outcomes.

Let's explore each one below.

1. The Director (Authoritarian: "Because I Said So")

The Director parent values order and compliance above all. They're known for setting clear rules with strict enforcement and maintaining high expectations with little room for flexibility. These parents are quick to correct and direct, believing that firm boundaries create responsible children.

The Director's approach brings notable strengths to the family dynamic. They excel at providing clear structure and setting high standards. Their consistent boundaries help children understand expectations, and they effectively teach respect for authority. These parents often run highly organized households where rules and consequences are clearly understood.

However, this style isn't without its challenges. The rigid nature of authoritarian parenting can create emotional distance in relationships, potentially discouraging independence as children grow. Power struggles often emerge as children naturally seek more autonomy, and emotional expression might be suppressed in favor of compliance.

2. The Friend (Permissive: "Whatever Makes You Happy")

The Friend parent prioritizes peace and harmony, often at the expense of structure. These parents typically establish few rules or consequences, preferring to avoid conflict whenever possible. They tend to rescue their children from difficult situations and protect them from natural consequences, believing that maintaining happiness is paramount to successful parenting.

This approach brings wonderful warmth to the parent-child relationship. These parents excel at creating strong emotional bonds, showing deep empathy, and maintaining open lines of communication. Children of Friend parents often feel deeply loved and emotionally supported, knowing they can always turn to their parents for comfort and understanding.

This style, however, faces its own set of challenges. Without clear boundaries, children might develop a sense of entitlement or struggle with self-discipline. The parent's tendency to rescue can enable dependent behavior, potentially undermining the child's ability to develop resilience and problem-solving skills.

3. The Guider (Authoritative: "Let's Figure This Out")

The Guider parent strikes a delicate balance between structure and flexibility. They set clear boundaries while remaining open to discussion and adaptation. These parents maintain high expectations while providing equally high levels of support, understanding that growth requires both challenge and nurture.

This balanced approach offers significant benefits. Guider parents excel at building strong connections while fostering independence. Their children develop robust problem-solving skills and emotional intelligence, learning to navigate challenges with confidence. The combination of clear expectations and emotional support creates an environment where children feel both secure and empowered.

The main challenge of this approach lies in its complexity. Being a Guider requires more time and energy than other styles. It demands consistent self-awareness and emotional regulation, along with the flexibility to adapt approaches based on the situation and the child's needs.

Your Parenting Style and the PCN Method

Understanding your natural parenting style is crucial to building your House of Harmony. It reveals your default responses under stress, highlights areas where you might need additional tools, and shows how your style might interact with your triggers. Most importantly, it helps identify patterns that could benefit from refinement.

 Remember: no parent operates purely in one style all the time. It's natural to flow between styles depending on stress levels, sleep quality, the day's challenges, which child you're dealing with, and what the situation demands. The goal isn't to completely transform your natural style—it's to enhance it with new tools that help you respond more effectively to your child's needs while honoring your own values and boundaries.

Ready to discover your parenting style? Let's begin.

The Parenting Style Quiz

What is your parenting style?

Respond to the following questions with your first instinct—try not to overanalyze. If you find yourself spending more than a few minutes on each, you may be overthinking. Aim for complete honesty, as your answers will provide insight into areas where you might want to adjust your approach with your children.

A) Most of the time B) Often C) Sometimes D) Almost never

1. I set strict rules and expectations for my child with little room for discussion.
2. I let my child do what they want without many limits.
3. I take time to explain the reasons for rules to my child.
4. I do not believe my child has the right to question my decisions.
5. I overlook misbehavior to avoid conflict with my child.
6. I listen to my child's opinion before making important decisions that affect them.
7. I lose my temper quickly when my child misbehaves.
8. I give in when my child throws a tantrum.
9. I apologize to my child when I make a mistake in parenting.
10. I discipline first and ask questions later.
11. I have trouble saying no to my child.
12. I take time to teach my child important life skills.
13. It is very difficult for me to cope when things are not the way I need them to be.
14. I don't like to interrupt my kids or bother others to do tasks that I can do for them.
15. I encourage my child to talk about their feelings.
16. I find I can do most tasks better than other people.
17. I let others have their way, even when I disagree.
18. I validate my child's thoughts and opinions.
19. I try to make sure things are done right the first time.
20. I fail to follow through on agreed-upon consequences.
21. I adjust rules and expectations as my child grows up.

This quiz was adapted from research on parenting styles, including the work of Diana Baumrind (1967) and later expansions by Maccoby and Martin (1983) and was generated on December 1, 2024, by ChatGPT, powered by GPT-4 Turbo.

Here's how to score your answers:

Mostly As = "Director," or Authoritarian style (Giving Orders)

Mostly B's = "Friend," or Permissive style (Giving In)

Mostly C's and D's = "Guider," or Authoritative style (Giving Choices)

Which one are you?

6

Putting Your New Perspective into Action – Your Bridge to Connection

"It's not what happens to you, but how you react to it that matters."

—Epictetus

N ow that you understand what shapes behaviors and responses, it's time to turn that knowledge into a new perspective and put it to action! This chapter shows you exactly how to use your new perspective in real situations, from morning meltdowns to sliding grades.

The Five Key Steps

You'll learn the five key steps that turn your new perspective into connection:

1. Understanding the Behavior
2. Checking Your Triggers
3. Applying Perspective
4. Using Perspective to Open Dialogue
5. Confirming Connection Through Reflection

Through Sarah's and Ashley's stories, you'll see how this process transforms challenging moments into opportunities for deeper understanding. Most importantly, you'll learn to recognize when you've made that crucial connection—your signal that you're ready to move from perspective to problem-solving in the *C* (Communication) phase.

The Power of the Pause

Pausing is a powerful way to give you a crucial moment and shift from reacting emotionally to responding thoughtfully using your perspective. Notice the use of the pause in the following two scenarios broken down into the five steps toward connection.

The Case of the Morning Chaos

Remember Sarah from the opening chapter? The mom who found herself locked in the bathroom, frustrated after another morning battle with her son over getting ready for school? Let's revisit that moment, but this time with your new perspective tools in place.

There she stands outside Jake's room, confronted by scattered clothes and a frustrated eleven-year-old insisting he can't find his "essential" blue shirt for his presentation. Her first instinct is to snap at him about responsibility and time management. But instead, she pauses to get her perspective lens on straight.

Step One: Understanding the Behavior

Sarah considers what she knows about Jake:

- He has a presentation today. *That's significant!*
- Why does he handle mornings like this? *Is he struggling with his organization?*
- He's been acting more defeated about school lately, which has me feeling helpless for him. *Is he displaying signs of inadequacy?*
- He's at an age where peer perception matters tremendously. *I remember those days.*
- He's never had to do a formal presentation before. *I can only imagine how anxious he must be.*

Step Two: Checking Your Triggers

Okay, so a lot could be happening with Jake right now. Is there anything going on with me too?

- *My heart is racing. I'm feeling that familiar tightness in my chest.*
- *I hate being late—that comes from my mom always making us feel terrible about tardiness.*
- *I'm worried about Jake being "irresponsible. What will the teachers or other parents think?*
- *I feel like his disorganization reflects on me, like I am a terrible mom for not teaching him better!*

Step Three: Applying Perspective

Sarah connects the dots: *Jake's behavior is possibly telling me he*

- *is feeling anxious about the presentation*
- *possibly feels overwhelmed by this new experience*
- *might be worried about what his classmates and teacher will think*

◆ *could be using the shirt as a way to express bigger feelings he can't name*

Step Four: Using Perspective to Open Up Dialogue

Instead of her usual emotional reaction of "Why didn't you get this ready last night?" Sarah takes a deep breath and chooses a different, more logical approach to respond rather than react:

◆ "Jake, I can see you're really worried about finding that shirt. Presentations can be nerve-racking. I remember feeling that way at your age too. Can you tell me what you're thinking about while we look for it together?"

◆ Jake's shoulders relax slightly. "What if I mess up? Jason and Mason never mess up. They'll probably make fun of me on the bus ride home if I make a mistake."

Step Five: Confirming Connection Through Reflection

Reflecting back what she hears, Mom validates what her son is saying. This allows Jake to feel truly heard and understood.

◆ "It sounds like you're really worried about messing up and being made fun of as a result." (reflection)

◆ "Am I right in that?" (confirmation)

When your child confirms your observations, you've made that vital connection. If not, maintain curiosity by asking questions, reflect back what you hear, and seek confirmation.

Jake's agreement here signals he feels truly heard and seen and is ready to move forward together with his mom.

The Result

This opens the door for a real conversation about anxiety, preparation, and courage—all while they locate the shirt (which was, indeed, in the laundry basket as Sarah had said, but now that discovery becomes about connection rather than correction).

Pro tip: Don't forget the power of the pause!

Picture this: Your son mutters, "You're so annoying," to his sister. Before you snap, "That's it, go to your room!" you pause. This moment—between trigger and response—is where parenting transformation happens.

As you learned in chapter 3, research in cognitive science and neuroscience suggests that the brain processes events in a sequence: a trigger sparks an automatic thought, which then creates an emotion and drives behavior. Most people jump straight to feeling and reacting, not paying much attention to the thought that started it all.

While you can't control that first automatic thought, you always have power over what comes next. A pause creates space between emotion and action, letting you shift from reaction to response. Instead of being driven by that first defensive thought, you can choose a perspective of understanding.

Need help finding the pause? Try this ten-second reset when emotions rise:

1. Take two quick deep breaths and slowly release.
2. Now notice what you're feeling (*I'm frustrated because I think they're being careless*).
3. Remind yourself, *My child is having a hard time, not giving me a hard time.*
4. Ask, *What else might be going on here?*

No time to pause? Remember from chapter 1, research in neuroplasticity shows that the brain strengthens pathways through repeated experience. Every time you practice emotional regulation, you reinforce neural connections, making calm responses more automatic over time. Meaning, the pause will begin to happen automatically—even during a crazy car ride when all your kids are talking at once!

Let's look at how this same process can work in another challenging situation.

The Case of the Slipping Grades

Ashley just received an email from fifteen-year-old Gia's teacher about missing assignments and dropping grades—something completely out of character for her typically conscientious daughter.

There she stands, holding the teacher's email, confronted by the reality of Gia's missing assignments and falling grades—something completely out of character for her typically conscientious fifteen-year-old. Her first instinct is to panic about her daughter's academic future. But instead, she pauses to get her perspective lens on straight.

Step One: Understanding the Behavior

Ashley considers what she knows about Gia:

◈ She is typically a conscientious student. *This sudden drop in performance is unusual.*

◈ She's fifteen and likely experiencing significant emotional or academic challenges. *What could be causing this change?*

◈ The teacher's email suggests a pattern of missing assignments. *Something must be impacting her usual approach to schoolwork.*

◈ Adolescence is a complex time with many academic and social pressures. *I need to understand her perspective.*

Step Two: Checking Your Triggers

Okay, so what's happening in Ashley's mind right now?

◈ *My heart is sinking. I'm feeling a mix of worry and frustration.*

◈ *I fear Gia might be falling behind academically. What if this impacts her future?*

◈ *I'm worried about being perceived as a "bad parent." Am I not supporting her enough?*

◈ *I have my own memories of academic pressure. I don't want to repeat my parents' reactive approach.*

Step Three: Applying Perspective

Ashley connects the dots: This isn't just about missing assignments. Gia's behavior is possibly telling her that

◈ *she might be experiencing emotional overwhelm or stress*

◈ *there could be potential challenges at school or with her social circle*

◈ *she needs support and understanding*

◈ *she's having difficulty expressing what's really troubling her*

Step Four: Using Perspective to Open Up Dialogue

Instead of emotionally reacting and criticizing, Ashely takes a deep breath and chooses a more compassionate approach:

- ◈ "Gia, I received an email from your teacher about some missed assignments. I'm concerned and want to understand what's going on. Can we talk about what might be making school-work challenging for you right now?"
- ◈ Gia's eyes well up. "I've been struggling with anxiety about my math class. I'm afraid to ask for help because I don't want to look stupid, but I'm falling behind, which makes me feel even more overwhelmed."

Step Five: Confirming Connection Through Reflection

Reflecting back what she hears, Mom validates what her daughter is saying:

- ◈ "It sounds like you're really having a hard time in math, and that is making you feel scared to ask. I can understand why that would be overwhelming." (reflection)
- ◈ "Am I right in that?" (confirmation)

When Gia confirms her observations, Ashley knows she has made that vital connection.

The Result

This opens the door for a real conversation about academic anxiety, support, and vulnerability. Gia feels heard and understood, creating a pathway for collaborative problem-solving.

What if connection is met with resistance?

Sometimes, teens might not be immediately open. If Gia had said, "I don't want to talk about it," Ashley would recognize this as a protective mechanism. Her response would remain steady: "I hear that you don't want to talk right now. That's okay. I'm here when you're ready."

Pro tip: The key is creating a space of unconditional support—an invitation, not an ultimatum.

You Are *Not* Ignoring the Problem by Waiting

When grades are slipping, every day matters. You might be thinking, *Who has time to wait?!* Here's the crucial point: taking time to build connection now isn't ignoring the problem; you'll address it directly in the next *C* (Communication) phase. Ashley isn't waiting passively; she's actively creating micro moments of connection using her perspective. These small investments compound quickly, moving you closer to the real conversations that lead to lasting change. This perspective-based approach transforms tension and fear into support and understanding, strengthening your relationship at a moment that could have pushed you apart.

The Power of Confirmation: Your Connection Checkpoint

Let's be honest: you're reading this book because you want to change challenging behaviors. You want the tantrums to stop, the grades to improve, the morning battles to end. So yes, it can feel frustrating to pause for connection when you're eager to solve the problem.

But here's the crucial insight: without confirmation that your child feels truly understood, any solutions you propose will likely be met with resistance. When your child says, "Yes, that's exactly how I feel," they're signaling they're ready to move from emotional reactivity to logical problem-solving.

Consider the following scenario.

> Parent: "Sounds like you're really frustrated with math."
>
> Child: "No, it's not that. The teacher moves too fast, and I'm embarrassed to ask questions."
>
> Parent: "Ah, so you're worried about looking confused in front of everyone; am I right?"
>
> Child: "Yes, exactly!"

That "yes" is your green light—the moment your child's brain shifts from defensive to receptive. Now you're ready for solutions that will actually stick. Skip this step, and you'll likely end up back at square one.

 Remember: Connection before correction isn't just a nice idea; it's your pathway to lasting change.

Perspective: The Foundation of PCN

As you can see, perspective transforms parent-child dynamics by shifting focus from surface behaviors to underlying needs. Rather than merely managing actions, it enables parents to understand what drives them. This is why perspective is the crucial first step—the foundation—in the PCN Method. Without it, you are just managing behaviors rather than meeting needs.

Like Ashley's situation with her daughter's grades, the visible struggle often masks deeper issues. When parents step back to gain perspective, they move from reactive questions (*Why won't she just listen?*) to responsive ones (*What support does she need?*).

This shift isn't about agreeing with the behavior; it's about creating the psychological safety children need to be vulnerable. Only when children feel truly seen can connection develop and real changes can be made. Perspective thus lays the essential groundwork for the entire PCN Method to succeed.

Now that you've learned to adjust your parental lens through perspective—seeing beyond behaviors to understand both yours and your child's true needs—you're ready to transform these insights into action. Like Jenny discovered with her daughter, Layla, what you focus on you feel. When Jenny stopped focusing on what Layla didn't do—her homework—and focused on what she did—helping her brother, Marco—Jenny felt better. This understanding creates connection, but it's what you do with that connection that builds lasting change.

As you move into exploring the *C*, or Communication, phase of the PCN Method, you'll learn how to leverage your newfound perspective to change behavior effectively with your children, whether through age-appropriate choices with younger ones or problem-solving partnerships with teens. Because once you can truly see your child's world, you can begin to work together to reshape it.

7

The Hidden Cost of Rushing to Fix – Why Connection Must Come First

"In order to change behavior, we must first engage the brain,
and we can only engage the brain through connection."

—Dr. Bruce Perry and Maia Szalavitz

Remember Ashley and Gia's story about the slipping grades? Ashley's first instinct was to lecture her daughter about responsibility and enforce strict study schedules. But jumping straight to solutions would have missed Gia's underlying anxiety about math—the real issue that needed addressing. As you are learning, behavior that looks like defiance often signals deeper struggles.

But before diving into the communication tools that will help you change challenging behaviors, there's something crucial to understand: what happens when we rush into problem-solving too quickly. Like building a house, you can't skip straight to putting up walls before laying a proper foundation. Yet that's exactly what most parents do, jumping into fix-it mode—lecturing, consequences, and solutions—before their child feels truly understood.

This chapter reveals the hidden costs of rushing to fix problems before establishing connection and shows you exactly how to recognize when you've built the foundation needed to make lasting changes. Because timing isn't just helpful—it's everything.

When Good Intentions Backfire

Research reveals two powerful forces driving parents to fix problems quickly: love and discomfort. When we see our child in distress, our own pain circuits activate. Parents rush to fix not just because they deeply want to help them but also because their distress makes them uncomfortable—and fixing feels like the fastest way to ease everyone's pain.

This fix-it impulse shows up in familiar ways, all born from good intentions: dismissing feelings ("You're fine!"), offering quick solutions ("I'll buy you a new one"), or jumping to lectures ("Well, if you had listened to me the first time . . ."). Sometimes parents even make their distress about themselves ("Why are you doing this to me?"), unconsciously trying to manage their own discomfort with their emotions.

But here's what happens when parents rush to fix before connecting—children respond in one of three ways:

5. They shut down and withdraw.
6. They fight back harder.
7. They comply on the surface while disconnecting inside.

That last one—surface compliance—feels like a win in the moment. Your child stops crying, says sorry, or does what you ask. But without feeling truly understood first, they're just going through the motions. Over time, this can lead to children who struggle to advocate for themselves, express emotions honestly, or maintain authentic connections.

Think of it like trying to bandage a wound without cleaning it first. The urge to stop the bleeding comes from love, and the rush to bandage comes from our own discomfort with seeing them hurt. But taking time to clean the wound properly, even though it might hurt more initially, shows deeper care for their long-term well-being.

The Pull of Patterns:
Why Parents Stay Stuck in Fix-It Mode

Humans are naturally drawn to patterns because they provide predictability and a sense of control in an uncertain world. Think of it like staying in an unfulfilling job—the discomfort you know feels safer than the uncertainty of change. Parents fall into the same trap with fix-it responses.

These fix-it patterns aren't just about avoiding discomfort either—they're deeply ingrained behavioral scripts, often passed down unconsciously through generations.

In *Parenting from the Inside Out* Dr. Daniel Siegel and Mary Hartzell (2004) explore how parents' childhood experiences shape their emotional responses, sometimes leading to automatic, unexamined reactions to their child's distress. Likewise, in *The Out-of-Sync Child* Carol Kranowitz (1998) highlights how early sensory and emotional experiences contribute to patterns of regulation and response. These ingrained habits can make "You're fine!" or "Just stop crying!"

an almost reflexive reaction—one that parents default to, even when they consciously want to respond differently.

This is especially powerful because these patterns often started as coping mechanisms in one's own childhood. If your emotions were consistently dismissed, you likely internalized this as "normal," making it your default response when faced with your child's distress. The fear of the unknown—of not having an immediate solution, of sitting with uncomfortable emotions, of potentially making things worse—can feel more threatening than sticking with patterns we know aren't working.

It's like being on a well-worn path through a forest. Even knowing there's a better route, stepping off that familiar trail triggers our brain's threat response. Just as someone might choose a difficult but predictable job situation over the uncertainty of finding a new one, we often stick with parenting patterns that don't serve us well.

The good news? Patterns can be broken. This is why simply knowing better isn't enough—parents need to build new patterns that feel as safe and reliable as the old ones, starting with the foundation of connection before correction. With practice and patience, these new patterns can become your default response, creating stronger connections with your children.

Recognizing Fix-It Mode: The "What the Heck" (WTH) Moment

Sometimes fixing works perfectly. Your child has a problem, you offer a solution, and they respond with "Thanks, that helps!" In these moments, there's no need to pause or reflect; you've matched your child's needs with the right timing.

But then there are those jarring "What the heck," or "WTH," moments, when your well-intentioned help backfires spectacularly. Consider this scene:

> Carol: "Your school project is still not finished? You're just not focusing enough. You need to put your phone down and just concentrate."
>
> Daughter: [*voice rising*] "You don't get it! I've been working on this for hours!"
>
> Carol: "Well, if you'd just follow the steps like I showed you . . ."
>
> Daughter: [*slams computer shut*] "You never listen!" [storms off, slams door]
>
> Carol: *I don't understand, I was just trying to help! WTH?!*

Science helps explain why these challenging moments happen: when children are emotionally overwhelmed, their ability to think logically becomes temporarily impaired. Siegel and Bryson's (2011) research on child development reveals that a child's brain fundamentally requires a sense of safety and understanding before it can effectively process solutions. Attempting to reason with a child in a heightened emotional state proves largely ineffective because their logical brain remains disengaged. Instead, connecting with their emotions first helps them regain neurological balance, making it easier to guide them toward constructive problem-solving.

In these heated moments, parents typically react in one of three ways: They fight back ("You will *not* speak to me that way!"), flee from the conflict ("I don't have time for this nonsense!"), or freeze

("Just look it up on YouTube!"). But none of these responses help your child feel connected enough to move from their emotional brain to their thinking brain.

Compare this to a more effective approach using connection:

Parent: "Get in the car—we're going to be late for soccer!"

Child: "No! I hate soccer! Everyone laughs at me!"

Parent: [*resisting urge to dismiss with "No one's laughing at you!"*] "Sounds like something about soccer is really bothering you . . ."

Child: "Yeah, last week Billy yelled when I missed the ball!"

Parent: "You're feeling hurt and maybe embarrassed when the other kids criticize your playing?"

Child: "Yes! Exactly!"

 Remember, if your child accepts guidance and moves forward happily, you've timed it right. But when your "help" sparks resistance or meltdown (WTH!), that's your signal to pause and switch from fix-it mode to connecting using your perspective.

Moving Forward: Getting to Solutions

By now you've learned the power of connection and why rushing to fix can backfire. But you're probably thinking, *This sounds great in theory, but I still need my child to get to soccer practice. Or finish their homework. Or clean their room. How do I actually make that happen?*

You're about to discover exactly that. The next chapter shows you how to move from understanding to action using communication tools that create real change. You'll learn specific strategies for common challenges like

- getting a resistant child to activities without yelling
- turning homework battles into productive work sessions without nagging
- moving from "I won't!" to "I'll try"
- building cooperation without bribes or threats

But here's what makes these tools different: they work with your child's brain instead of against it. Once you've established connection through perspective (confirmed by that crucial "Yes, that's exactly how I feel!"), your child's thinking brain comes back online. Now they're ready not just to hear solutions but to help create them. This self-determination will help to instill these changes for the long haul! Until then, resist the urge to jump straight to problem-solving, a.k.a. "fix-it mode," even when the clock is ticking.

 Remember: the bridge to lasting change isn't built on quick fixes; it's built on connection first.

8

The Communication Phase – Moving from Connection to Change

"Children must be taught how to think, not what to think."

—Margaret Mead

You've built the foundation through perspective: staying regulated, understanding behaviors deeply, and creating true connection through reflection and confirmation and staying out of "fix-it mode." Your child now feels seen, heard, and understood.

Now comes the moment you've been waiting for: turning that connection into change. With your child's brain receptive and ready to learn, you can address their need for self-determination through effective communication strategies.

This chapter introduces communication skills that evolve with your family, providing tools you'll use from toddler tantrums through teen challenges. Get ready to learn strategies that build lasting cooperation while strengthening your parent-child bond.

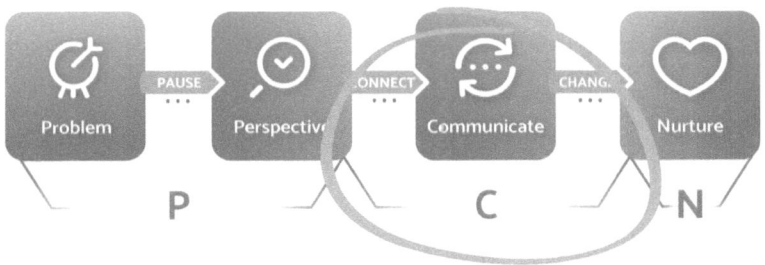

Understanding Your Role as Teacher

Many parents use discipline to enforce compliance often through punishment or control. Here's a crucial insight: *discipline*, according to the *Online Etymology Dictionary*, comes from the Latin word *disciplina*, meaning "instruction" or "teaching" (Harper n.d.). This transforms your role from punisher to educator. When parents approach discipline as education rather than punishment, children develop crucial life skills like self-control and responsibility. They learn to make good choices not from fear of consequences but from understanding and internal motivation.

Think of discipline like teaching bike-riding. You don't punish falls; you support balance. Similarly, when your child rolls their eyes or lashes out, your job isn't to hand down consequences but to teach alternatives—i.e., better ways to express frustration, vocabulary for big feelings, tools for emotional regulation. This is yet another perspective shift that can change the outcome of your parenting: defiant moments become teaching opportunities. A tantrum signals time to teach emotional skills. Even a meltdown offers chances to demonstrate coping strategies.

When in doubt, ask yourself,

◈ *What lessons do I want to teach my children?*
◈ *What do I want my children to learn from this?*
◈ *Do I want them to learn from fear or genuinely want to improve?*

The Hidden Price of Fear-Based Discipline

Fear-based discipline works; that's why so many parents use it. Threats, harsh consequences, and punishment can stop unwanted behaviors quickly. A child who loses privileges or faces stern punishment learns what not to do, and fast.

But studies on fear-based discipline methods by Siegel and Bryson (2011) reveal the steep cost. When parents discipline through fear, they activate their child's survival instincts. It's the same defense mode—fight, flight, or freeze—that you feel when triggered, and it makes learning impossible. Instead of developing problem-solving skills or emotional regulation, they just learn to avoid punishment. This creates surface compliance but leaves them without tools to handle similar situations better next time.

The long-term impact runs deep. Children raised with fear-based discipline often struggle with low self-esteem from constant criticism and poor emotional regulation since they never learned healthier ways to cope. They tend to have difficulty trusting authority figures and solving problems independently. Many develop a tendency to lie or hide mistakes rather than learn from them.

In contrast, children taught through supportive discipline develop confidence, self-control, and problem-solving abilities. They learn to trust their parents as guides, not just enforcers. Most importantly, they gain the emotional tools needed for lifelong success.

The choice is clear: you can force compliance through fear or build skills through teaching as a disciplinarian. One works immediately but costs dearly; the other takes patience but creates lasting change.

Understanding Discipline Through Self-Determination

Maya slumped into her chair, unzipping her backpack with more force than necessary. She was about to start her college applications, had the computer application program right open on her desk, when her mom walked in from work.

"Time to get those college essays done!"

Just like that, Maya's motivation evaporated. She hadn't even realized she was rolling her eyes until she caught her mom's sharp intake of breath.

"Excuse me? That attitude isn't acceptable, young lady."

And there it was: the familiar dance of resistance and reaction, each feeling disrespected by the other. Maya, frustrated that her mom assumed she needed reminding about her college essays she was already planning to do. Her mom, hurt by what she perceived as defiance rather than what it really was: her daughter's natural need for autonomy.

This scene plays out in countless homes, but there's fascinating science behind why. According to Dr. Edward Deci and Richard Ryan's (1985) research on the Self-Determination Theory highlights that humans have a core psychological need for autonomy—the feeling of having some control over one's life. When this need for autonomy is disrupted or restricted, even unintentionally, people instinctively resist or push back.

Think about it: have you ever been about to do something—load the dishwasher, make a phone call, start a project—only to feel instantly resistant when someone tells you to do it? That's your own need for self-determination in action.

The good news? Understanding this need transforms how we communicate with our children. In this *C* phase, you'll discover two powerful approaches that honor your child's need for autonomy while maintaining necessary boundaries:

1. For younger children, the art of offering choices
2. For older children, the power of collaboration

Both techniques share a crucial foundation: they invite children into the decision-making process, building what researchers call "autonomous motivation"—the internal drive to make positive choices not because they are being told to but because they want to.

While involving children in decision-making builds crucial life skills, it's important to remember two key principles:

1. Safety always comes first. There are always nonnegotiable boundaries around health, safety, and core family values.
2. Collaboration doesn't mean capitulation. The goal is teaching children how to think through decisions, not giving them complete control. Parents remain the ultimate authority while guiding children toward increasingly independent decision-making as appropriate for their age and maturity.

How You Say Things Matters More Than What You Say

The approach you use when communicating with your child can either invite cooperation or trigger resistance, often having a greater impact than the words themselves.

For Younger Children (approx. <10 years): The Power of Choice

Young children experience countless moments each day where they feel powerless, when they're told when to wake up, what to wear, what to eat, when to sleep. It's no wonder they often push back with "No!" or "I don't want to!" But research from Dr. Ross Greene (1998) shows that when children feel they have some control over their world, challenging behaviors decrease dramatically.

The key lies in how we frame these choices. Instead of asking, "Do you want to clean up?" (which invites a "no"), try "Would you like to clean up the blocks first or the trucks?" This simple shift preserves your child's sense of autonomy while maintaining necessary boundaries.

Consider eight-year-old Thomas and his nightly battle over reading time. His mom used to announce, "Time to read!" only to face immediate resistance. After learning about self-determination, she shifted to "Would you like to read in your bed or the cozy chair?" and "Should we set the timer for fifteen or twenty minutes?" Suddenly, reading time transformed from a power struggle into a collaborative experience.

For Older Children (approx. >10 years): The Art of Collaboration

As children enter their tween and teen years, their need for autonomy intensifies. Research shows that the adolescent brain is specifically wired to seek independence and resist authority. This isn't defiance; it's development.

Remember Maya from the opening story? Imagine if instead of directing her about college essays, her mom had opened with curiosity: "It looks like you haven't started your essays yet. If that's the case, what's your plan to get started? I know it can feel overwhelming to start." This approach acknowledges Maya's growing independence while creating space and respect for genuine dialogue about responsibilities.

The magic of collaboration lies in its respect for the teen's perspective. When fourteen-year-old Alex kept forgetting to take out the garbage, his dad resisted the urge to impose restrictions. Instead, he invited Alex into problem-solving: "It looks like you are not holding up your end of the household responsibilities, but I believe you can do better. What ideas do you have?" Together, they developed a chores schedule that worked for both of them—not because Dad demanded it but because Alex helped create it.

This isn't about letting children do whatever they want. It's about finding that sweet spot where your guidance meets their growing need for independence. When parents communicate in ways that honor self-determination, they do more than solve immediate challenges; they help children develop the internal compass they'll need for life.

Let's see how else this looks in real life:

> Four-year-old Max stands firm, arms crossed: "No! I don't want to brush my teeth!" His dad, remembering the importance of choice, shifts approach: "Would you like to brush your teeth in your bathroom or mine?" Max's resistance melts: "Yours!"

> Fifteen-year-old Sophie slams her bedroom door: "You can't make me go to rehearsal!" Her mom, using collaboration instead of control: "You're right; I can't make you. But I'm curious what's making rehearsal feel so hard right now?" Sophie pauses, door cracking open: "I don't even know where to start."

Mom: "It sounds like something's really bothering you about rehearsal. Let's figure out a solution together that works best."

The magic in both these moments isn't just about avoiding power struggles. It's about meeting that fundamental need for self-determination in age-appropriate ways. For young Max, simple choices give him a sense of control within safe boundaries. For Sophie, collaborative problem-solving honors her growing need for autonomy while maintaining parental support.

The Power of Self-Determination

Dr. Carol Dweck's research in *Mindset: The New Psychology of Success* (2006) highlights that when children participate in age-appropriate decision-making, they develop essential life skills such as emotional regulation and problem-solving. This involvement nurtures a growth mindset, encouraging them to see challenges as opportunities for learning and development, which supports long-term success.

Think of it like teaching your child to cook. Parents can either do all the cooking themselves while children watch, leave them alone in the kitchen to figure it out, or create structured opportunities to learn—starting with simple tasks like stirring, progressing to following recipes, and eventually planning full meals. This balanced approach builds confidence while maintaining safety and support, helping children develop their own "inner compass" for decision-making.

But fostering self-determination doesn't mean giving children complete kitchen freedom. Instead, it means offering appropriate choices within clear boundaries. A younger child might choose which vegetable to prepare, while a teenager helps plan weekly menus. Their voice in decisions sparks a natural drive to cooperate and contribute.

This approach transforms daily challenges into opportunities for growth. Rather than forcing compliance, you're building internal motivation that leads to lasting change. Your child learns not just what to do but how to think through decisions independently. Choice and collaboration become essential tools in your parenting tool kit, creating not just immediate cooperation but the foundation for lifelong decision-making skills.

The Right Words at the Right Time by Age

Just as you wouldn't hand car keys to a toddler or use baby talk with a teenager, your communication approach needs to match your child's developmental stage. The words you choose can either build cooperation or trigger resistance. Understanding which phrases to use—and which to avoid—transforms daily interactions from power struggles into opportunities for growth. Below is your practical guide to age-appropriate communication.

Structured Choices (Ages 2–9): Limited, clear options that give younger children appropriate control

Keys to Effective Choices
- Offer two to three options, all acceptable to you.
- Make choices clear and specific.
- Use positive framing.
- Keep choices to the present and relatable to the event you want changed.

Examples in Action

- ◈ "Would you like to put your shoes on inside the house or in the car?"
- ◈ "Should we clean up using the timer or the cleanup song?"
- ◈ "Do you want to shut the TV off or have me do it?"

Examples to Avoid

- ◈ "What do you want to wear?" (too open-ended)
- ◈ "Do you want to clean up?" (yes/no questions invite resistance)
- ◈ "Would you rather clean your room or go to bed?" (ultimatums are ineffective)

Real-Life Scenarios

- ◈ Morning Rush: Instead of battling over breakfast, try, "Would you like cereal in the blue bowl or oatmeal in the red bowl?"
- ◈ Bedtime Resistance: Rather than "Go to bed now!" try, "Should we hop like bunnies or tiptoe like mice to bed?"
- ◈ Getting Dressed: When your child insists on wearing their superhero costume to school, try, "You can wear your cape for ten minutes before we leave or save it for after school; which works better?"

Collaborative Problem-Solving (Ages 10+): Partnership-based approaches that respect older children's emerging autonomy

Keys to Effective Collaboration

- ◈ Invite their input first.
- ◈ Listen more than you speak.
- ◈ Focus on joint problem-solving.

◈ Maintain boundaries while showing flexibility.
◈ Continue to stay connected through reflecting and confirming if things go astray.

Examples in Action
◈ "What ideas do you have for managing your schedule?"
◈ "How can we make this homework routine work better for you?"
◈ "What support do you need from me? I am available until it's time to make dinner."

Actions to Avoid
◈ Solving the problem for them
◈ Dismissing their ideas without discussion
◈ Taking full control when partial independence would work

Real-Life Scenarios
◈ Screen Time Conflicts: Instead of imposing rules, try, "I notice you're frustrated with the current screen time limits. What adjustments would help you manage your time better?"
◈ Homework Struggles: When grades slip, start with "Help me understand what makes this subject challenging for you. What resources might make it easier?"
◈ Messy Room: Rather than demanding cleanup, try, "What system could we set up to help you keep your space organized in a way that works for you?"

A Note on Development and Flexibility

Every child develops at their own unique pace. While this guide suggests age ranges for different communication approaches, you know your child best. Feel free to

- ❖ use choices with older children if they are having a hard time coming up with their own ideas for solutions
- ❖ try collaboration with mature younger children
- ❖ mix approaches based on the situation
- ❖ adjust language complexity for your child's understanding level

The goal is finding what works for your specific child and family, not rigidly following age guidelines.

The Bridge Between Ages: When and How to Transition

As children mature, their need for autonomy grows along with their capabilities. The transition from structured choices to collaborative decision-making should happen gradually, matching their development. Watch for signs of readiness: your child might show interest in planning activities, make thoughtful choices in small matters, seek more independence, or clearly explain their reasoning when making decisions.

Keep in mind that the goal isn't perfection; it's building decision-making muscles through practice. Your role evolves from director to mentor, providing a safety net while letting your child test their judgment. This balanced approach builds confidence and competence, preparing them for increasingly complex choices ahead.

Don't Forget Your Foundation: A Clear Perspective Before Communication

Think back to the last time you tried reasoning with your child while feeling frustrated. Maybe you offered choices through gritted teeth or attempted collaboration while anxiety about their grades twisted in your stomach. How did that work out?

 Remember: Perspective isn't just about seeing your child's behavior differently—it's the lens through which communication flows. When you're emotionally triggered, even the most perfectly worded choices or collaborative approaches can sound like demands or threats to your children.

Picture Betty, exhausted after work, finding her son's backpack full of lunch trash and scattered garbage. Without a pause for perspective, she might snap, "Clean this up now or lose video games!"

But with a quick reflection (*He's been struggling with organizing tasks lately. What support does he need?*), she shifts to say, "I notice the lunch cleanup has been tricky. Would setting a reminder or creating an afterschool checklist help you remember?"

When perspective guides your parenting choices, you stay calmer while setting limits, listen more authentically during discussions, and maintain boundaries without emotional reactions. Your focus shifts from controlling behavior to teaching skills, keeping your long-term parenting goals in mind.

This mindset transforms daily challenges into learning opportunities. Rather than demanding immediate compliance, you're building lasting capabilities. Instead of triggering pushback, you're creating cooperation. Your child learns not just what to do but how to think through situations, developing skills they'll use for life.

Most importantly, perspective keeps you anchored in your teaching role when emotions run high. It reminds you that each interaction shapes not just today's behavior but tomorrow's capabilities.

 Remember: Pause, reflect, *then* communicate.
Your perspective sets the tone for success.

Your Feelings Matter Too

Let's be honest: watching your child struggle or act out can feel like a punch to the gut. That pit in your stomach when you see them lose a football match, the frustration bubbling up during the fifth argument about screen time, or the anxiety that spikes when your toddler or the anxiety that spikes when your toddler has yet another meltdown when they're told no about another snack.

These feelings? They're valid. They're human. They're part of caring deeply about your child's well-being. But remember, when a parent leads a conversation with raw emotions, they unintentionally flip the script. Or as I like to think of it, emotions can lead to more emotions.

Here's why this matters. As adults, we've experienced both sides: being young and growing older. But our kids? They're navigating childhood's complex emotions for the first time. Expecting them to manage their own feelings while simultaneously processing and responding to ours is like asking someone to learn to swim while carrying another person. Wouldn't you rather have your child use their natural desire to please you and make you proud because they feel secure and connected to you? Or do you want them to become people-pleasers by suppressing their own growth just to manage your emotions?

For example, a teen might rush through homework sloppily just to ease your visible anxiety, rather than learning effective study habits. A young child might stop expressing frustration altogether to avoid triggering your anger, rather than learning healthy emotional expression.

So does this mean you should bottle up your feelings? Absolutely not. The key is expressing them in a way that teaches rather than transfers emotional burden. The "When, Then, Because" method preserves your voice while keeping the focus on learning.

The "When, Then, Because" Method: A Bridge Between Feelings and Teaching

The "When, Then, Because" method, introduced by Dr. Ross Greene (1998), is a communication strategy that helps children connect their actions to consequences in a clear and empathetic way. Rooted in behavioral psychology, it encourages understanding and collaboration by explaining the "why" behind actions, fostering cooperation, and promoting intrinsic motivation without shaming or overwhelming the child.

The "When, Then, Because" method also transforms how parents share their feelings with their children. Rather than overwhelming children with their parents' emotions, this approach creates clear connections between actions and their impact.

When you say, "When you jump on the couch," you're naming a specific behavior without judgment. Adding "then someone could get hurt" shows the direct consequence. Finally, "because furniture isn't made for jumping" completes the learning connection. This three-part structure keeps conversations focused on understanding rather than blame or shame.

Think of it as building a bridge between your feelings and your child's learning. Instead of "Your messy room is driving me crazy!" (which puts your emotions at the center), you might say, "When clothes are left on the floor, then it's harder to keep the house clean because the vacuum can't reach the carpet." Now your child understands the impact without feeling responsible for managing your emotional state.

This method works because it maintains your authority while respecting your child's developing ability to understand cause and effect. It also naturally leads into problem-solving: once everyone understands the "why," finding solutions becomes collaborative rather than combative.

Examples of using "When, Then, Because" in Choice/ Collaboration Communication Practice

Younger Children

Before: "Stop screaming! You're giving everyone a headache!"

After: "When you scream inside, then it hurts our ears because sound echoes off the walls. Should we use our 'indoor voice' or go outside to yell?"

School-Age Kids

Before: "Your closet is a disaster! I'm tired of finding crumpled clothes everywhere!"

After: "When clothes get crumpled in your closet, then clothes get lost because it's hard to find what you need. Would a basket system or separate pouches work better?"

Teens

Before: "I'm so stressed about your social plans. Don't you even care about my social life?"

After: "When you make plans without asking me first, then I feel overwhelmed because it feels extra hectic for everyone involved. What planning system might help us keep track of your social calendar?"

Using "When, Then, Because" transforms teaching moments in a profound way. Rather than rushing to fix behavior to ease a parent's distress, children learn to genuinely understand the impact of their actions. They develop solutions based on real understanding rather than from a place of guilt or emotional burden.

This reframe also helps children understand natural consequences and develop intrinsic motivation, rather than practicing just to ease their parents' stress about wasted money. The emphasis stays on learning and growth while acknowledging parental investment in a constructive way.

Building Life Skills Through Choice and Collaboration

When children participate in decisions, they develop crucial skills that shape their future. Consider homework routines. While "No screens until homework's done!" might achieve temporary compliance, asking, "What's your ideal homework setup?" helps children create systems they'll actually follow. This shift from external control to internal motivation transforms daily challenges into growth opportunities.

Through collaborative problem-solving, children develop essential capabilities: managing time and emotions, creating solutions rather than just following rules, understanding consequences, and building confidence through successful experiences. These skills emerge naturally as children practice making choices within safe boundaries.

This approach strengthens family bonds by replacing power struggles with partnership. Instead of enforcing rules, parents guide children toward better decisions. Trust deepens as children feel heard and respected, while communication channels stay open even during challenging years.

Research shows the lasting impact: children raised with choice and collaboration demonstrate stronger emotional regulation, better academic performance, and more satisfying relationships. They develop greater independence and decision-making abilities that serve them throughout life.

Remember: Each conversation isn't just about solving today's challenge—it's about building tomorrow's capabilities. The more families practice collaborative communication, the more natural it becomes for everyone involved.

Transforming Communication Roadblocks into Opportunities

The words we choose can either invite collaboration or shut down dialogue. "I think you should" tells children their input isn't needed. "But" erases everything said before it, signaling that their feelings matter less than the solution. Even seemingly collaborative phrases like "Don't you think . . ." or "Wouldn't it be better if . . ." subtly push your agenda.

Replace these barriers with genuine curiosity:

"What feels most challenging right now?"

"What would make this task more manageable?"

"How do you think we could solve this?"

These questions invite children to analyze situations and participate in solutions. Each conversation becomes an opportunity to develop critical thinking and problem-solving skills rather than just achieve compliance.

 Remember: When you drop directive phrases for curious questions, you're not just getting better cooperation today; you're building your child's capacity for independent thought tomorrow.

"I've Tried This Before and It Doesn't Work!"

Many parents hesitate to embrace communication this way because previous attempts haven't delivered the promised results. Perhaps you've tried giving choices, only to have your child demand options outside the boundaries you've set. Or maybe you've attempted collaboration with your teen, but the conversation devolved into negotiation or arguing.

Often, what seems like failed choices or collaboration stems from subtle miscalculations in our approach. A parent might offer choices when their child is already emotionally flooded, present too many options that overwhelm their child's decision-making abilities, or inadvertently phrase choices as threats ("Either do your homework now or lose your phone"). Others jump straight to problem-solving ("fix-it mode") before establishing emotional safety and connection.

Consider Nancy, who tried collaborating with her fourteen-year-old about putting away her sports equipment after practice: "Let's figure out a storage system and routine that works." But she launched this conversation right after an argument about dirty cleats, when neither she nor her daughter were emotionally regulated. Or David, who gave his six-year-old "free choice" at bedtime without clear boundaries, creating chaos rather than cooperation.

These are classic WTH moments signaling missing steps in the PCN Method. Success with choices and collaboration requires the following:

- ❖ Clear perspective: are you regulated enough to guide this process?
- ❖ Genuine connection: does your child feel emotionally safe and understood?
- ❖ Developmental matching: are your expectations aligned with your child's capabilities?
- ❖ Proper timing: is everyone calm enough for productive discussion?

 Remember: research shows that the brain becomes more receptive to guidance when feeling seen, not safe and understood. Attempting problem-solving before establishing emotional connection typically triggers defensive responses, blocking cooperation.

Previous struggles with choices and collaboration don't predict future failure; they highlight opportunities to strengthen your foundation of perspective and connection first.

Building Changes That Last

Picture Reilly, age thirteen, slumped at the kitchen table struggling with social studies homework. Two months ago, this scene would have ended in tears and slammed doors. But today is different. Her mom, Brianne, pauses, remembering to check her perspective before speaking. Instead of jumping in with solutions, she asks, "What part feels hardest right now?" Reilly looks up, surprised at the space to voice her frustration. Together, they identify the challenge and brainstorm study strategies that work for Reilly's learning style.

This transformation didn't happen overnight. It came from consistently applying the communication tools you've learned here: maintaining clear perspective, offering age-appropriate choices, collaborating on solutions, and using "When, Then, Because" to express impact without emotional burden. Through these practices, Reilly isn't just learning math; she's developing critical thinking skills that will serve her long into adulthood.

The journey of connected communication is exactly that—a journey. Some days you'll nail it, offering perfect choices and collaborating like a pro. Other days you'll catch yourself in the middle of saying, "I think you should . . . ," and need to course-correct. That's not just okay; it's part of the process.

As you move into the next chapter on nurture, the *N* portion of the PCN Method, you'll discover how to sustain these positive changes through clear boundaries and consistent practices. You'll learn specific strategies for keeping your home harmonious even when challenges arise, and how to adapt your approach as your children grow. Because the goal isn't perfect parenting; it's creating lasting connection while helping your children develop the skills they need for life.

 Remember: Every conversation is an opportunity to either strengthen or strain your connection. Choose your words thoughtfully, lead with perspective, and trust in the power of collaborative communication to build lasting change.

9

Keeping Your House of Harmony Sturdy with Nurture

"I've learned that people will forget what you said, people will forget what you did, but people will never forget how you made them feel."

—Maya Angelou

Picture a house you've worked hard to build. The foundation is solid, the walls are strong, but without a protective roof, everything inside remains vulnerable to life's storms. This is where many parents find themselves after working through the first two phases of the PCN Method. They've developed a fresh perspective (*P*) on their children's behavior and learned to communicate (*C*) with choices and collaboration. Yet without the final element of nurture (*N*), these positive changes may not weather the challenges ahead.

In this chapter, you'll discover how nurture serves as the protective roof of your House of Harmony, creating the safety and consistency that allow everything else to thrive. More importantly, you'll get a clear road map for the practical nurturing skills you'll explore in the coming chapters—essential tools that will help you maintain and strengthen the positive changes you've already made to grow with you and your family for the long haul.

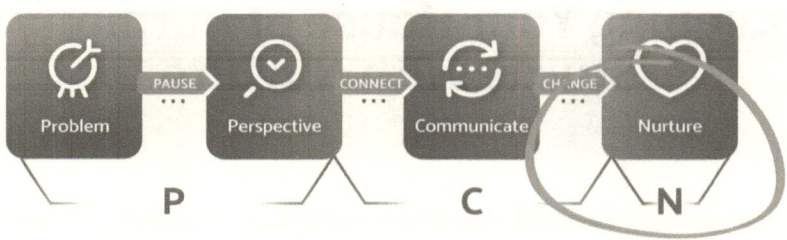

Understanding Safety:
The Science Behind Nurture

Imagine telling your child they can have screen time after finishing their homework. Your child completes the assignment, but you're in the middle of an important call when they come to collect on your promise. Despite the inconvenience, you honor your word because you understand something crucial: your child is learning about trust through every interaction. This moment isn't just about screen time; it's about your child learning they can rely on your word.

Dr. Stephen Porges's (2011) research on the nervous system, particularly through his polyvagal theory, reveals that children's brains are constantly assessing their environment for safety or threat. When parents consistently demonstrate reliability through their words and actions, they help create the foundation of trust essential for a child's development.

This reliability isn't about always saying yes; it's about children knowing they can count on their parents' word, whether the answer is yes or no.

Trust develops when parents follow through on their statements and maintain consistent boundaries. For example, when a parent says they will attend their child's school performance, showing up demonstrates reliability. Similarly, when they say a behavior will have a specific consequence, following through builds trust. This predictability allows children's nervous systems to relax, enabling them to focus on learning and growing rather than questioning their environment's reliability.

Porges's (2011) research shows children's brains continually assess three key questions:

1. *Am I safe?*
2. *Can I predict what's coming next?*
3. *Do I have someone steady to rely on?*

When children can confidently answer yes to these questions through consistent parental nurturing, their brains shift from survival mode to learning and growth mode. This scientific understanding explains why nurture through reliability and consistent boundaries creates the environment necessary for the *P* and *C* elements of the PCN Method to flourish.

The Art of Nurturing: Flexible Tools for Your New Toolbox

Just as a skilled builder doesn't rely on a hammer for every job, effective parenting requires knowing when and how to apply different nurturing tools. These five nurturing practices are like essential tools in your new parenting toolbox—each serving a unique purpose to keep your family feeling safe and being appropriate to the situation at hand.

Think of the following five nurturing practices as specialized tools, each designed for specific scenarios.

1. **Boundaries and Follow-Through: Your Structural Tool (to be discussed in chapter 10)**

Like a level that ensures a building stands straight, boundaries create the essential structure children need. However, just as a level might be too rigid for curved surfaces, some situations call for flexible boundaries:

   ◈ High-stakes situations—where safety issues require firm, unwavering boundaries

   ◈ Learning opportunities—where new experiences might need more flexible boundaries

   ◈ Emotional moments—where boundaries sometimes need temporary adjustment while maintaining core principles

2. **Encouragement vs. Praise: Your Growth Tool (to be discussed in chapter 11)**

Imagine encouragement as scaffolding and praise as a prop. While praise may provide temporary support, encouragement, like scaffolding, is designed to foster growth and can be gradually removed as your child develops their skills:

   ◈ Achievement moments—Focus on effort and strategy rather than innate ability.

   ◈ Challenging times—Emphasize perseverance and learning from mistakes.

   ◈ Daily activities—Notice and acknowledge small steps of progress.

3. **Effective Consequences vs. Punishment: Your Teaching Tool (to be discussed in chapter 12)**

Think of this as choosing between a chisel and a sledgehammer. While punishment is a blunt instrument aimed at controlling behavior, effective consequences are a precise tool that helps guide learning by teaching the natural outcomes of actions.

- Natural consequences—the natural outcomes of a child's actions, such as getting wet after playing in the rain without a rain jacket. These teach children about cause and effect in a real-world context.
- Logical consequences—directly linked to behaviors, designed by the parent to show the connection between the action and its outcome. For example, if a child refuses to do their homework, the logical consequence might be missing out on a fun activity later because they didn't complete their responsibilities.

4. **Strategic Use of Rewards: Your Motivation Tool (to be discussed in chapter 13)**

Like using temporary supports in construction, rewards can be helpful when used strategically:

- New skill development—Temporary rewards can jumpstart positive habits.
- Challenging transitions—Short-term rewards can ease difficult changes.
- Long-term goals—Gradually fade rewards as internal motivation develops.

5. **Parental Self-Awareness: Your Measuring Tool (to be discussed in chapter 14)**

Like a measuring tape that ensures accuracy, self-awareness helps you gauge your responses:

- Emotional triggers—Recognize when your past experiences affect your reactions.
- Stress responses—Understand how your state influences your parenting.
- Growth opportunities—Use mistakes as chances to model learning and accountability.

When you consistently apply these nurturing practices, you're doing much more than managing behavior—you're creating a foundation of security and trust. Your child learns that they can count on you, that your words have meaning, and that your love remains constant even during challenging moments.

These five nurturing practices aren't just techniques—they're your pathway to preserving and strengthening the positive changes you've worked so hard to achieve in the previous *P* and *C* phases. Each practice, when applied with consistency and care, reinforces the message that you're a dependable source of both support and structure in your child's life—aka *safety*! By maintaining this delicate balance through these nurturing tools, you protect and nurture the growth you and your child have already accomplished together.

The Art of Adaptation

Mastering these parenting tools takes practice and flexibility, much like a builder adapting to changing conditions. In future chapters we'll dive deeper into these tools and show you how to use them in different situations. But for now, be ready to adjust your approach based on the following variable:

- ◈ **Context.** Since the context of each situation matters greatly, what works for homework battles may not resolve sibling conflicts, and strategies effective at home might need modification in public settings.
- ◈ **Your child's developmental stage and individual temperament.** These should guide your approach, as should your family's unique values and culture. (Refer back to *"What Shapes Behavior"* in chapter 4)

- ◈ **Your child's current emotional state.** If they're overtired, hungry, or particularly sensitive, be mindful of your own energy levels and available resources.
- ◈ **Complexity levels.** Complex interventions require more bandwidth than simpler approaches, so match your strategy to both the situation and your capacity.
- ◈ **Environmental factors and time constraints.** These will naturally influence your choices, but always keep your long-term parenting goals in sight to ensure your adaptations align with your overall vision for your child's development.

Understanding Your Family's Patterns

 Remember in chapter 7 when you learned about how brains are always looking for patterns? It's just like how you know exactly what your coffeemaker will do each morning, or how you can predict what your partner will say when you mention takeout for dinner again. These patterns provide a sense of safety and security by offering predictability—you know what to expect. Even when the anticipated outcome is unpleasant, the certainty itself can be reassuring.

Your kids are doing the exact same thing with you—they're pattern-seeking experts! Watch them for a minute and you'll see it: they know that leaving LEGO on the floor usually gets an eye roll from you, while leaving their coat on the floor is met with frustration. They've figured out that asking for screen time right after homework tends to work better than asking during dinner. They're not being manipulative; they're just really good at noticing what to expect from you.

Here's the thing that might make you pause: even your not-so-great reactions can become patterns your kids count on. Maybe your child has learned that if they push hard enough, you'll eventually give in about bedtime. Or perhaps they know that the third "Mom!" is when you finally look up from your phone. Even the challenging patterns give them a sense of "at least I know what's going to happen."

When Good Intentions Create Challenging Patterns

Meet David, who came to my office concerned about his fifteen-year-old son, Michael. "I don't understand what's happening," he sighed. "I've always tried to make things easier for him. I handle all his school emails, I track his assignments, I even help him draft texts to teachers when he needs extensions. But now? He blows up if I don't immediately respond to his texts about homework questions. He won't even check his own grades online; he just waits for me to tell him what's missing."

David described a recent evening when Michael had a history project due. "He came home at eight o'clock after hanging out with friends, assuming I'd already emailed his teacher about an extension. When I suggested he email the teacher himself, he slammed his bedroom door and yelled that I never help him when he really needs it. I lost it and started shouting about how ungrateful he was, how I manage his entire academic life, and he can't even be bothered to check his own assignment due dates!"

As David spoke, I helped him see the pattern that had developed. Like many caring parents, he wanted to protect Michael from academic stress. But by managing everything, he'd created a pattern where Michael expected instant solutions and hadn't developed his own problem-solving skills.

We explored how this pattern, while predictable, wasn't preparing Michael for college or life. Yes, Michael could count on Dad to handle everything school-related, but this pattern was preventing him from developing responsibility, resilience, and independence.

Your Family's Safety Check: A Practical Exercise

As you begin implementing the nurturing practices you're exploring, start by observing your family's current patterns. Consider these key areas:

Predictability Patterns

Notice what happens when

- ◈ your child asks for screen time
- ◈ siblings have a conflict
- ◈ someone spills something
- ◈ homework time arrives
- ◈ bedtime approaches

Emotional Weather Patterns

Observe how

- ◈ your responses change when you're tired versus energized
- ◈ your boundaries shift based on whether you've had a good or bad day
- ◈ your morning rules differ from your evening rules
- ◈ your children behave when they sense you're stressed versus calm

Boundary Patterns

Consider whether

- ◈ you follow through consistently on limits
- ◈ your children understand the difference between safety rules and preferences
- ◈ you're rigid about small things but inconsistent with bigger issues
- ◈ you say no at first but give in after pressure

Connection Patterns

Notice if

- ◈ your children come to you when upset or hide their struggles
- ◈ you react emotionally versus respond thoughtfully
- ◈ your children expect understanding or punishment when things go wrong
- ◈ your children test limits more during times of stress

What You'll Achieve Through Nurture

"I used to believe that being a good parent meant giving my kids everything I never had growing up," shares Maria, mother of three teens. "But I've learned it's more about being dependable and following through with what I say. My kids actually trust me more now because they know what to expect, even if they don't always like it."

By embracing these nurturing practices, you'll witness powerful transformations for both you and your child. Your child will develop stronger emotional regulation, feel more secure in testing boundaries appropriately, and build resilience in facing challenges. For you, this means a shift from exhausting power struggles to meaningful connections, from constant correction to collaborative growth, and from reactive parenting to confident leadership.

As you begin exploring each nurturing practice in the coming chapters, you'll receive clear examples, practical strategies, and solutions to common challenges. You'll learn not just the "what" but the "how" of nurturing parenting—specific techniques that create the safety your family needs to thrive.

Just as a strong roof protects everything beneath it, these nurturing practices will safeguard the progress you've made with perspective and communication. You're not just learning individual skills; you're creating an environment where growth happens naturally and learning feels safe. This is the true power of the *N* in the PCN Method: it transforms your house into a true home where everyone can flourish.

 Remember: Consistency within the PCN Method isn't just about teaching specific skills; it's about creating an environment where your entire family can thrive through predictable, nurturing interactions.

10

Building Your Protective Framework – The Power of Boundaries and Follow-Through

"Daring to set boundaries is about having the courage to love ourselves, even when we risk disappointing others."

—Brené Brown

"I can't keep doing this," Elena sighed, slumping into her office chair during our session. Her eyes were tired, her shoulders tense. "Every night it's the same dance with my kids. I say it's bedtime, they beg for more time. I say no screens after dinner, but somehow they're always back on their tablets. When I try to enforce rules, they throw tantrums. So I give in just to keep the peace, but then I feel awful because I know I'm teaching them not to take me seriously."

Elena's struggle reflects a challenge many parents face: understanding the importance of boundaries while finding it nearly impossible to maintain them consistently. As we reviewed patterns earlier in chapter 9, Elena later found herself caught in one that wasn't serving anyone—her children had learned that persistence would eventually break down her resolve, leaving her feeling increasingly powerless and resentful.

Understanding Boundaries: More Than Just Rules

Before diving into Elena's journey, let's clarify what boundaries really mean. At their core, boundaries are clear limits and rules that define what behaviors are acceptable. But they're so much more than just a list of dos and don'ts. Think of them as the invisible lines that create safety in relationships—like the walls of a house, they provide structure and protection while allowing freedom within their confines.

Imagine a playground next to a busy street. Without a fence (boundary), children play cautiously, staying close to the center, their play inhibited by uncertainty and fear. But with a secure fence in place, these same children run freely, laugh loudly, and explore every corner of the space. The boundary hasn't restricted their freedom; it's actually created the security needed for true freedom to emerge.

Healthy boundaries form the essential framework within which families can thrive, acting like the walls of a well-designed home that keep everyone safe while allowing room to grow. Many parents worry that setting firm boundaries will create conflict or distance in their relationships, but the opposite proves true. Clear, consistent boundaries actually reduce anxiety for both parents and children by eliminating the exhausting cycle of negotiation and uncertain consequences.

Think of boundaries as your family's operating manual. They answer essential questions:

- What behaviors are acceptable in our family?
- How do we treat each other? How do we want to be treated?
- What are our expectations around safety, respect, and responsibility?
- What happens when someone crosses a boundary?
- How do we repair relationships when mistakes happen?

When children understand this operating manual, they can relax into its predictability. It's like having a clear map for a journey; even if parts of the path are challenging, knowing the route reduces stress and builds confidence. Parents, too, find relief in having established guidelines, eliminating the need to make decisions about limits and consequences in the heat of the moment.

Within this framework of security, children develop the confidence to explore their emotions and independence, understanding that adults will guide them before situations become unsafe. Mistakes transform into learning opportunities rather than sources of shame, as children experience a balanced approach of accountability paired with understanding.

Most importantly, consistent boundaries build a foundation of trust between parents and children, creating a reliable environment where everyone can focus less on testing limits and more on growing together. This predictability becomes the bedrock of family harmony, reducing power struggles and creating space for deeper connection.

Keep in mind, when parents struggle to set clear boundaries, children often have difficulty accepting them. As you begin implementing changes, it's common for children to resist—this push-back is a normal part of their adjustment process. However, as discussed, patterns can be changed, and consistency is key to those changes.

Types of Essential Family Boundaries

Every healthy family needs different types of boundaries to create a secure and nurturing home environment—much like a house needs various structural elements to stand strong. Below are the key boundaries that work together to protect both individual needs and family harmony.

Physical Boundaries

- Personal space and body autonomy
- Safety rules about touching others
- Expectations around private versus shared spaces
- Guidelines for physical play and roughhousing

Emotional Boundaries

- Expression of feelings in appropriate ways
- Respect for others' emotional states
- Privacy and consent in sharing personal information
- Balance between independence and family connection

Time Boundaries

- Daily routines and schedules
- Screen time limits
- Boundaries between work/school and family time
- Age-appropriate bedtimes

Social Boundaries

- Rules about interaction with peers
- Online behavior expectations
- Family time versus individual time
- Respect for others' relationships

When these boundaries work together, they create the secure foundation your family needs to thrive. Like a well-tended garden, these protective elements allow your perspective (*P*) and communication (*C*) skills to take root and flourish into lasting family harmony.

How Boundaries Reinforce Positive Change

Imagine you've worked with your child to create a new morning routine, complete with choices about breakfast and clothing selection. This represents wonderful progress in communication and cooperation. But what happens when your child tests these new agreements? Without clear, consistent boundaries, the message becomes muddled: *Sometimes Mom means what she says, and sometimes she doesn't.* This uncertainty can actually increase anxiety and resistance, undermining the positive changes you've made.

When children experience consistent boundaries alongside improved communication, they learn several powerful lessons: their parents' words have meaning, agreements made together are meant to be honored, changes aren't just temporary fixes but new ways of living, their choices come with real responsibilities, and trust goes both ways—they can trust your consistency, and you can trust their growing capability.

Think of boundaries and limits as the container that holds all your other positive parenting efforts in place. Just as a glass holds water and gives it shape, boundaries provide the structure that allows your improved perspective and communication to take meaningful form in daily life. Without this container, even the most wonderful changes can slip away like water through your fingers.

 Remember: your children are constantly learning whether your words match your actions. When you combine clear communication with consistent boundaries, you're teaching them that what you say matters. This reliability creates the security they need to fully embrace the positive changes you're making together.

The Root of Boundary Struggles

If you've ever stood in a grocery store while your child melts down over a denied candy request, feeling everyone's eyes on you . . . If you've caught yourself giving in to "just five more minutes" of screen time for the fourth time today, even though you promised yourself you wouldn't . . . If you've lain awake at night wondering if you're being too strict or too lenient, replaying your parenting decisions and second-guessing every choice . . .

Then you understand how setting and maintaining boundaries with children can feel like navigating an emotional minefield—even when you intellectually grasp their importance.

This struggle isn't a sign of parental failure; rather, it reflects the complex interplay of one's past experiences, present emotions, and deeper psychological needs that emerge in the parent-child relationship.

Six Common Boundary Challenges

1. *The Impact of Our Own Childhood:* Your childhood experiences create an internal blueprint that guides your actions. Parents who grew up with overly rigid boundaries might swing to the opposite extreme, while those raised with few limits might struggle to create structure.

   Key insight: Your "emotional inheritance" shapes your comfort level with authority.

2. *The Attachment Factor:* Your biological drive to maintain connection with your children can make their emotional responses to boundaries feel threatening. When a child protests a limit, it triggers a parent's protective instincts.

   Key insight: Discomfort with your child's boundary-related distress is natural but shouldn't guide your decisions.

3. *Modern Parenting Pressures:* You are parenting in an era of unprecedented information and scrutiny. Social media comparisons and conflicting advice can erode confidence and lead to inconsistent boundary-setting.

   Key insight: External pressure often creates internal doubt about legitimate boundaries.

4. *The Reality of Parental Exhaustion:* When you're depleted, maintaining consistent boundaries requires energy you might not have. This can lead to "decision fatigue," where you choose the path of least resistance.

   Key insight: Your capacity for boundary-setting is directly linked to your self-care.

5. *Cultural and Family Influences:* Extended family members might criticize your choices, and different cultural perspectives

on discipline can create internal tension about appropriate boundaries.

Key insight: Align your boundaries with your family's values while respecting cultural influences.

6. *The Weight of Emotional Labor:* Parents often carry grief about setting limits, especially when boundaries trigger memories of their own childhood disappointments. This emotional weight can manifest as guilt or over-explanation of boundaries.

Key insight: Your emotional response to setting boundaries often reflects deeper personal history.

By understanding these challenges, you can begin to separate your children's temporary disappointment from your deeper fears about relationship damage. This awareness transforms how you view both yourself and your children during challenging moments—bringing us back to the power of perspective.

Understanding Your Current Blueprint

Before creating lasting change with boundaries, it's essential to understand your starting point. Consider these key questions about your boundary-setting patterns. Don't aim for perfect answers; instead, use this reflection to identify your strengths and areas for growth.

Take a moment to reflect on the following factors and questions.

Your Past Influences

◈ How did your own childhood experience with boundaries shape your current parenting style?

◈ Do you find yourself either repeating or deliberately doing the opposite of how you were parented?

Your Emotional Response

◈ What emotions arise when you need to enforce a boundary with your child?

◈ How do you handle your child's disappointment or protest when maintaining limits?

Your Current Challenges

◈ Which boundaries do you find most difficult to maintain consistently?

◈ What typically causes you to give in after you've set a limit?

◈ How does exhaustion or stress affect your boundary-setting abilities?

Your Support System

◈ How aligned are you and your co-parent (if applicable) on boundaries?

◈ What pressures do you feel from extended family or your community about your parenting choices?

Take note of patterns in your responses. Do you notice yourself struggling more with boundaries when tired? Do family opinions make you second-guess your choices? Does your child's emotional response trigger difficult feelings from your own childhood? Understanding these patterns isn't about judgment; it's about identifying where you might need extra support or strategies as you strengthen your boundary-setting skills.

 Remember: Every parent brings different strengths and faces different challenges with boundaries. Your awareness of these patterns is the first step toward positive change.

Finding Self-Compassion Through Understanding

Understanding these deeper roots of boundary-setting challenges is crucial for developing a more compassionate and effective approach. When you recognize that your struggles often stem from love, protection, and deep emotional experiences rather than weakness or incompetence, you can begin to address them more constructively.

This awareness allows you to separate your children's temporary disappointment from your deeper fears about relationship damage or emotional harm. Moreover, gaining insight into your boundary struggles transforms how you view both yourself and your children during challenging moments—aka perspective!

As you have learned, perspective can create a powerful ripple effect throughout your parenting journey. And parents who understand the source of their boundary challenges often report seeing their children's behavior in a new light. When you can comprehend why maintaining boundaries feels so challenging, you're better equipped to prepare for difficult moments, develop effective coping strategies, and maintain emotional equilibrium when your children push back against limits.

Reframing Boundaries as Love

As a reminder, struggles with boundaries often stem from a place of deep love. When you give in to "just five more minutes" of screen time or hesitate to enforce a consequence, it's usually because the emotional pull overrides your logical understanding of long-term outcomes. This is a sign that you need to adjust your perspective.

Instead of viewing boundaries as restrictions, try changing your perspective and seeing them as one of the most loving gifts you can offer your child. When you maintain consistent boundaries, you're teaching your child they can count on you, showing them how to navigate life's natural limits, providing the security they need to grow confidently, and modeling healthy relationship skills they'll carry into adulthood.

Just as you wouldn't feel guilty about installing a safety gate at the top of the stairs for a toddler, you don't need to feel guilty about maintaining other boundaries that keep your child safe and help them grow. Consider these powerful outcomes of consistent boundaries:

For Your Child

- ◈ Develops trust in your words and actions
- ◈ Learns to respect and set their own healthy limits
- ◈ Builds emotional resilience through managing disappointment
- ◈ Gains confidence in navigating clear expectations

For Your Family

- ◈ Creates predictable, calm routines
- ◈ Reduces power struggles and negotiations
- ◈ Strengthens parent-child connection through consistency
- ◈ Establishes a foundation of mutual respect

 Remember: Every time you maintain a loving boundary, you're not just managing behavior; you're building your child's sense of security, capability, and trust in themselves and you. That's something to feel good about!

Elena's Journey: The Power of Consistent Boundaries

Six months after our initial session, Elena returned with a different energy. "I wish I could go back and tell myself what I know now," she shared, smiling. "Remember how every night used to be a battle? Now my kids know that when I say, 'Screens off at seven thirty,' that's exactly what happens—no negotiations, no extra minutes, no drama."

The transformation hadn't been easy. Elena had to face her own discomfort with setting limits and work through her fear of being the "mean parent." She learned to recognize that her children's protests against boundaries weren't signs of relationship damage but normal testing behaviors that actually signaled their need for consistent limits.

"The biggest change came when I realized that following through on boundaries wasn't about punishing my kids. It was about teaching them to trust my word and, ultimately, to trust themselves," Elena explained. "Now when I say something will happen, it happens. No endless warnings, no negotiations, no yelling needed."

The impact extended beyond bedtime routines. Her children began showing more responsibility with homework, responding better to daily limits, and even starting to set their own boundaries. Most surprisingly to Elena, her relationships with her children deepened rather than suffered. "I was so afraid that being firm with boundaries would make them resent me," she reflected. "Instead, they seem more secure, more cooperative, and actually more affectionate. It's like they finally know exactly where the lines are, so they can relax and just be kids."

Your Blueprint for Growth

The journey toward better boundaries isn't about achieving perfection—it's about creating a strong foundation for your family's growth and well-being. Just as Elena discovered, each small step toward consistency builds trust and security that transforms your family dynamics. Success begins with focusing on one boundary at a time, maintaining it consistently even when faced with protests, and remembering that testing limits is both normal and temporary.

You'll know you're making progress when your words and actions align more consistently, power struggles decrease as expectations become clear, and your confidence in setting limits grows stronger. Watch for signs that your child is beginning to trust and respect boundaries more readily, and notice how you feel more peaceful about maintaining limits. These subtle changes signal important shifts in your family's dynamic.

Your commitment to creating loving, consistent boundaries is one of the most powerful gifts you can give your children. Trust that even on challenging days, you're laying the groundwork for their future success and emotional well-being. Remember Elena's transformation—the path to better boundaries may not always be easy, but the results are worth every step of the journey.

11

Understanding Encouragement – Building Inner Strength for Lasting Change

"Tell me and I forget. Teach me and I remember. Involve me and I learn."

—Benjamin Franklin

Think of confidence like a sturdy bridge your child will cross countless times throughout their life. While praise might add a fresh coat of paint to this bridge, making it temporarily shine, encouragement strengthens the underlying structure itself.

This chapter explores how to move beyond surface-level praise to build that essential foundation of inner strength and resilience. As you've built your House of Harmony through perspective and communication, adding consistent boundaries, you've created the secure environment where encouragement can take root. Now it's time to learn how your words can nurture growth that lasts long after the successful communication changes made in the previous stages have been made.

Why Words Matter More Than We Think

Meet Denise, who came to my office worried about her thirteen-year-old daughter, Victoria's, sudden reluctance to try new things. "I don't understand what happened," Denise shared. "I'm always telling her how smart she is, how talented. But lately, she gives up at the first sign of difficulty. Last week, she quit her science project because it wasn't 'perfect enough.' She used to love science!"

As we explored Denise's approach, a pattern emerged. Like many caring parents, she believed she was building Victoria's confidence through constant praise: "You're so brilliant!" "You're the best in your class!" "Everything you do is amazing"!" But Victoria had internalized a different message, that her worth depended on being "perfect" and "the best." The pressure to maintain these labels was paralyzing her willingness to take risks or face challenges.

Denise's story illustrates why the way we speak to our children matters so deeply. This isn't surprising when we consider how encouragement differs from praise. While praise focuses on results and innate abilities ("You're so smart!"), encouragement recognizes effort and builds resilience ("You worked hard to figure that out!"). Encouragement nurtures a mindset that supports long-term growth and persistence. Children who receive consistent encouragement are more likely to keep going when faced with challenges, recover from setbacks, try new approaches, and maintain positive changes over time.

This distinction makes encouragement a crucial complement to boundaries in your House of Harmony. While boundaries provide the external structure your child needs to feel secure, encouragement develops their internal resources, turning temporary progress into lasting change.

Let's explore.

The Key Difference: Praise vs. Encouragement

Many parents believe they are encouraging their children when they offer praise, but these two approaches have fundamentally different impacts on child development. The key distinction lies in what each method focuses on: praise centers on the child's traits, while encouragement addresses the child's efforts and behaviors.

Understanding Praise: Focus on the Person

Praise puts the spotlight directly on the child by

- labeling personal qualities ("You're so smart!")
- emphasizing natural talents ("You're a gifted athlete!")
- creating fixed identities ("You're my artistic one!")
- setting up expectations ("You're always so good!")

The Hidden Challenges of Praise

While praise might seem like a natural way to build confidence, it often creates unintended pressure that can actually inhibit growth. When children receive constant praise about being "smart," "talented," or "the best," they often feel compelled to maintain these labels at all costs.

This burden can make them hesitant to attempt new challenges where they might not excel immediately. Their sense of worth becomes tied to maintaining their "special" status, leading to an unhealthy dependency on others' approval rather than developing internal motivation. Even simple mistakes can feel threatening to their identity when they believe their value comes from being "perfect" or "naturally gifted."

Over time, this praise-dependent mindset can significantly reduce a child's willingness to take risks or venture into areas where they might initially struggle, limiting their potential for growth and learning. The very words intended to build them up can inadvertently create barriers to their development.

Understanding Encouragement: Focus on the Process

While praise puts the spotlight on the person, encouragement puts the spotlight on actions and efforts by

- noticing specific behaviors ("You studied consistently all week.")
- acknowledging strategies ("You tried different approaches until you found what worked.")
- recognizing effort ("You kept working even when it was difficult.")
- highlighting progress ("You're getting more comfortable with these problems.")

The Benefits of Encouragement

Unlike praise, encouragement cultivates a mindset that supports long-term growth and resilience. When children receive consistent encouragement, they develop internal motivation that drives them to pursue goals for their own satisfaction rather than external approval. They learn to value their effort and persistence, understanding that improvement comes through practice and dedication rather than innate talent alone.

This shift in perspective helps them approach challenges as opportunities for growth rather than threats to their identity. As they experience the positive feedback loop of effort leading to progress, they naturally develop stronger problem-solving skills and greater confidence in their ability to overcome obstacles.

Most importantly, encouragement helps children view mistakes not as failures but as valuable stepping-stones toward mastery, creating a willingness to tackle new challenges with optimism and determination. This growth-oriented mindset becomes the foundation for lifelong learning and resilience.

Common Praise Statements vs. Encouragement Alternatives

Praise	→	Encouragement
"You're so smart!"	→	"You found an effective way to solve that problem."
"You're the best player!"	→	"Your practice is really showing in your game."
"You're such a good girl!"	→	"You considered how your actions would affect others."
"You're a natural artist!"	→	"You're experimenting with different techniques."
"You're always so helpful!"	→	"Your help with setting the table made dinner run smoothly."

Think about a recent time you praised your child. How could you rephrase it as encouragement? What specific effort or strategy could you acknowledge?

How Encouragement Nurtures Long-Term Change

As we explored in chapter 8, Dr. Carol Dweck's (2006) research on developing a growth mindset reveals how children who believe they can grow through effort achieve more than those who view their abilities as fixed.

When children hear encouragement focused on process ("You found a creative solution") rather than traits ("You're the smartest"), they develop resilience that helps them maintain positive changes. This growth mindset becomes essential as they face new challenges, helping them view setbacks as natural stepping-stones rather than failures. This mindset is crucial for maintaining the changes you've worked so hard to create with your child.

Can I Never Praise My Child Again?

There's nothing wrong with celebrating achievements or expressing genuine joy in your child's accomplishments. The key is making encouragement your primary approach, focusing on behaviors and efforts rather than personal qualities. Instead of "You're the strongest one on your team," try "You found a really effective way to overcome your fears and score that touchdown. What strategy did you use?"

This subtle shift in language transforms moments of success from pressure to maintain a label into opportunities for growth and learning. By balancing occasional praise with consistent encouragement, you create an environment where your child feels both celebrated and supported in their continued development.

Why Encouragement Sustains Change

When children understand precisely what they did well, they gain a clear road map for future success rather than relying on vague compliments about their character or abilities. Encouragement naturally focuses on specific efforts that children can repeat, turning each success into a learning opportunity rather than pressure to maintain a label. This approach steadily builds their confidence in handling challenges because they recognize that their achievements come from their actions and choices, not from fixed traits they must protect.

Unlike praise, which can create dependency on others' approval, encouragement develops internal motivation as children learn to value their own growth and effort. Perhaps most importantly, when children receive consistent encouragement, setbacks begin to feel less threatening because they understand that every challenge, whether met with immediate success or temporary struggle, offers a chance to learn and grow stronger.

> **Pro tip:** Want to really boost your child's self-esteem? Turn the tables and ask them to encourage themselves!

When your child accomplishes something or works through a challenge, ask questions like these:

- ◈ "Why are you proud of yourself right now?"
- ◈ "What did you do differently this time that worked better?"
- ◈ "How did you help yourself keep going when it got hard?"

This self-encouragement is powerful because it teaches children to recognize their own growth and build internal standards for success. Dr. Martin Seligman (1998), a prominent figure in positive psychology, shows through his research that the ability to self-reflect and self-encourage is one of the strongest predictors of long-term resilience and success.

Encouragement in Action: The PCN Method

Think about the difference between praise and encouragement in your PCN journey. When your child makes progress with communication skills, you might be tempted to say, "You're such a good communicator now!" While this praise feels good momentarily, it creates pressure to maintain a label.

Instead, try encouragement: "I noticed how you expressed your feelings clearly while also listening to understand mine. What helped you do that?" This approach helps your child identify specific behaviors they can repeat and build upon.

As you continue your PCN journey, focus on noticing and supporting effort, progress, and specific behaviors. Below are some additional ways to focus on encouragement.

Encouraging Phrases

"I appreciate you taking the time to sit and collaborate with me. I know it's not always easy for you to communicate your problems."

"I know how much thought you put into your solutions. I am proud of the effort you put in. Are you proud of yourself too?"

"I know you're disappointed. What do you think you can learn from this experience? What are you willing to try next time?"

Discouraging Phrases to Avoid

"Why would you say something like that? That's not what we agreed on."

"I knew you wouldn't follow through with our collaboration. You never listen!"

"I am so tired of putting in all this hard work just to deal with your drama."

The encouraging statements above express empathy, reassurance, and faith in your child's capability even during challenging times, while the discouraging statements undermine self-esteem through criticism and disappointment. By choosing encouragement over criticism, you help your child build the internal resources they need for lasting growth. Which would motivate you more to change?

Remember Denise and Victoria? As Denise learned to encourage Victoria's process rather than praise her intelligence, changes began to emerge. When Victoria faced a challenging math problem, instead of saying, "You're so smart, you'll figure it out!" Denise tried, "This is a tough problem. What strategies have worked for you before that have helped?"

The result? Victoria started approaching challenges differently. "Mom, this is hard, but I'm going to try breaking it down like I did last time." She was developing resilience and problem-solving skills rather than fearing failure.

Encouragement: The Gift That Builds Inner Strength

Think of encouragement not as a parenting technique but as a gift you freely give your child. Unlike praise, which children must earn through performance or achievement, encouragement is uncondi-tional—supporting growth and building confidence regardless of outcome. This shift in perspective transforms how we interact with our children during both successes and struggles.

 When in doubt, remember it this way: when parents believe in their children, they help children believe in themselves!

Consider these five powerful gifts when remembering to use encouragement:

1. *The Gift of Internal Motivation.* When encouragement comes without conditions, children learn to pursue goals for their own satisfaction rather than external approval. Instead of ask-ing, *Will this make Mom proud?* they begin to ask themselves, *What do I want to learn from this?*

2. *The Gift of Resilience.* By encouraging effort rather than out-come, we help children develop the emotional strength to bounce back from setbacks. They learn that challenges are opportunities for growth, not threats to their worth.

3. *The Gift of Authentic Self-Esteem.* Unlike the fragile confidence built through praise, encouragement helps children develop genuine self-worth based on their efforts and growth. They learn to value themselves not for being "the best" but for being persistent, curious, and willing to learn.

4. *The Gift of Problem-Solving Skills.* When we encourage rather than rescue or praise, children develop confidence in their

ability to handle challenges. They become active participants in their own growth rather than passive recipients of others' judgments.

5. *The Gift of Emotional Regulation.* Through encouragement, children learn that all emotions and efforts are acceptable, even when they don't lead to perfect outcomes. This helps them develop healthy ways to handle disappointment and frustration. Each word of encouragement you offer is another small gift contributing to their developing sense of capability, resilience, and self-worth.

Building on Encouragement

Consider encouragement as one of the essential tools in your nurturing tool kit. Along with the boundaries we discussed in the previous chapter, encouragement creates an environment where your child feels secure enough to grow, change, and learn from mistakes. When you combine clear boundaries with consistent encouragement, you create the perfect conditions for lasting positive change.

In the next chapter, we'll explore another crucial aspect of nurturing: the difference between consequences and punishment. You'll discover how to implement consequences that teach rather than just penalize, maintaining the encouraging, growth-focused environment you're creating. Just as encouragement builds internal motivation, effective consequences help children develop responsibility and learn from their choices.

Your journey through the PCN Method is building layer upon layer of positive parenting skills. Each new tool you add—from perspective to communication, from boundaries to encouragement—strengthens your ability to nurture lasting change in your family. As you move forward, keep practicing encouragement in your daily interactions. The more natural it becomes, the more you'll see your child's confidence and resilience grow.

12

Effective Consequences vs. Punishment

"Where did we ever get the crazy idea that in order to make children do better, first we have to make them feel worse?"

—Dr. Jane Nelsen

To ultimately nurture all the new changes in the **P** and **C** phases of the PCN Method, children need to understand that their actions have direct results, both positive and negative, through consequences. These cause-and-effect experiences form the foundation of human learning from early childhood through adulthood.

Understanding Consequences

Consequences come in two distinct forms, each playing a crucial role in child development:

> **Natural consequences** stem directly from a child's actions without parental intervention. When a child refuses to wear a coat, they feel cold. When they don't complete homework, their grades suffer. When they spend all their allowance immediately, they can't buy something they want later. These automatic outcomes teach valuable life lessons through direct experience.

> **Logical consequences,** by contrast, are thoughtfully designed to relate directly to behavior. Unlike natural consequences that happen automatically, logical consequences are appropriate, related outcomes that help children learn from their choices. For instance, consistently misusing phone time during homework hours might result in losing phone privileges during study time. Or if a child continues to use their markers to draw on the wall, they lose their marker time. These consequences make sense because they directly connect to the choice made.

The Key Difference: Consequences vs. Punishment

The fundamental distinction between consequences and punishment lies in their purpose and approach to behavior change.

While punishment operates from a place of authority and focuses on making children suffer for their mistakes, consequences create opportunities for learning and growth. When parents rely on punishment, they often impose penalties focusing solely on past mistakes rather than future choices. For example, a punishment might be taking away a child's phone for a week because they were disrespectful. This approach typically breeds resentment, damages the parent-child relationship, and teaches children to act from fear rather than understanding.

Consequences take a fundamentally different approach. They're typically discussed and agreed upon in advance, creating clarity and buy-in from both parent and child. Rather than being arbitrary, consequences maintain a direct, logical connection to the behavior in question. Another example would be a child losing bike privileges for a day after repeatedly forgetting to put it away. This approach shifts the focus from past transgressions to future choices, helping children understand the natural relationship between their actions and outcomes. Perhaps most importantly, consequences maintain the crucial connection between parent and child, preserving the relationship while teaching responsibility.

The effectiveness of consequences stems from their alignment with real-world cause and effect. When children experience logical consequences for their choices, they develop a deeper understanding of how their actions impact their lives and the lives of others. This natural learning process helps build internal motivation and responsibility, rather than teaching them simply to avoid punishment or please authority figures.

The Timing of Consequences: Why Order Matters

Remember what you learned in chapter 7 about the brain's readiness for solutions in "fix-it mode"? Traditional parenting often jumps straight to consequences assuming the emotional brain is ready for problem-solving.

"Clean your room or lose your phone!" "Do your homework or no video games!" "Be home by curfew or you're grounded!" While these statements might seem logical, remember, they skip crucial steps in how the brain processes change. And as you discovered earlier, the brain follows a specific sequence when processing challenges. The emotional brain must feel safe and understood before the logical brain can engage with solutions and consequences!

Let's revisit the brain's sequence using a common scenario. Your teenager comes home an hour past curfew. The traditional approach might immediately announce, "You're grounded for a week!" But consider what's happening in both your brain and your teen's brain at that moment. You're likely feeling worried and angry; they're probably feeling defensive and anxious. Neither of you is in a brain state conducive to learning or problem-solving.

Research from the field of neuropsychology confirms this sequence. Perry and Szalavitz's (2006) studies show that the brain physically cannot engage in problem-solving or learn from consequences while in a state of emotional distress. It's like trying to install new software while your computer is overheating—it simply won't work effectively.

This explains why consequences alone often fail to create lasting change. When parents skip the essential steps of perspective (*P*) and communication (*C*), they're essentially trying to teach a lesson to a brain that isn't ready to learn. But when consequences follow connection through perspective and self-determination through communicating with choices and collaboration, they become powerful tools for growth rather than sources of resentment.

So remember, just as you wouldn't start building a house with the roof, you should never start behavior change with consequences unless there was a safety concern. The foundation of perspective and the walls of communication must come first. This sequence ensures that when consequences are implemented, they fall on receptive ground, ready to nurture real learning and lasting change.

Pro tip: Get children invested in their own consequences!

The most effective consequences aren't those we impose on our children but those we develop *with* them. This collaborative approach directly taps into that core human need for self-determination that you learned about in the *C* phase. When children participate in determining their own consequences, they gain a sense of control over their lives, which promotes critical problem-solving skills and helps them develop what psychologists call an "internal locus of control"— the understanding that their choices directly affect their outcomes. Rather than just reacting to punishments, they learn to think through consequences, which set them up for success in making thoughtful decisions throughout their lives.

Remember this core truth: People invest more deeply in solutions they help create. This approach develops confident decision makers who understand their power to shape their own path.

The Power of Collaborative Consequences: A Real-World Example

Consider thirteen-year-old Marcus, who struggled with completing his homework before video games. His mother had tried everything: taking away devices, grounding him, limiting screen time. Each punishment led to arguments, sneaking games, and damaged trust. During a family therapy session, Mom tried something different. Instead of his mother setting the consequences, she asked Marcus, "What do you think would help you remember to finish homework first?"

After some thought, Marcus suggested that if he played games before completing homework, he would lose gaming privileges for the next week. This was actually stricter than what his mother had been imposing, but something remarkable happened: Marcus started consistently doing his homework first. When asked why this consequence worked better, he explained, "It feels fair because I came up with it. And I know exactly what will happen if I make the wrong choice."

Think about how differently these conversations sound. If you were a kid, which one would motivate you for long-term change?

Traditional "Fix-It Mode" Approach

> Parent: "If you don't clean your room right now, I'm donating all your LEGO toys!" Or "You lied about where you were! You're grounded for two weeks with no phone!"

Collaborative Approach

> Parent: "If you can't keep your LEGO toys organized, what should happen to ensure they don't get lost or

broken?" Or "When you weren't honest, it damaged our trust. What privileges should be earned back as trust grows?"

Safety First

As mentioned earlier, safety issues always require a different approach. Nonnegotiable rules about seat belts, fire safety, or dangerous behavior need firm, parent-determined consequences. However, even here, parents can involve children in understanding why these rules matter.

> Parent: "Seat belts are nonnegotiable because they save lives. But I'm curious, why do you think some people choose not to wear them?"
>
> Child: "Sometimes they're uncomfortable."
>
> Parent: "I understand that. What ideas do you have for making it more comfortable while staying safe?" Or, "I get it. I feel uncomfortable too sometimes, so how can we make it fun? Do you want to buckle in like a race car driver or like a spaceship pilot today?"

This approach serves multiple important purposes: it acknowledges your child's perspective while maintaining clear boundaries, involves them in problem-solving rather than simply enforcing rules, and builds genuine understanding rather than mere compliance. Together, these elements help children learn not just what the consequences are but why they matter.

Five Key Reasons Consequences Work

1. *Teach cause and effect:* Children naturally learn from outcomes tied to their actions, building an understanding of how choices shape results. This mirrors real-world experiences, like forgetting an umbrella leading to getting wet.

2. *Encourage internal motivation:* Logical consequences shift the focus from external control to internal regulation. When children collaborate in creating consequences, it activates brain areas tied to impulse control and decision-making, fostering psychological ownership (Siegel and Bryson 2011).

3. *Promote emotional regulation:* Consequences allow for learning in a calm, receptive state. Perry and Szalavitz's (2006) research shows the brain cannot process lessons effectively when in emotional distress, making validation and collaboration essential steps before implementing consequences.

4. *Strengthen self-regulation and decision-making:* Children who experience logical, consistent consequences are more likely to develop better self-regulation, improved judgment, and a stronger sense of accountability. This approach helps them understand the connection between their actions and the outcomes, fostering skills that contribute to responsible decision-making and emotional growth.

5. *Build trust and connection:* When parents implement consequences collaboratively, it reduces power struggles and resentment. This approach preserves the parent-child relationship while teaching critical life skills.

By focusing on agreed-upon consequences, parents guide their children toward learning responsibility and understanding the natural impact of their actions, creating a foundation for lifelong growth and independence.

Putting It All Together with the PCN Method

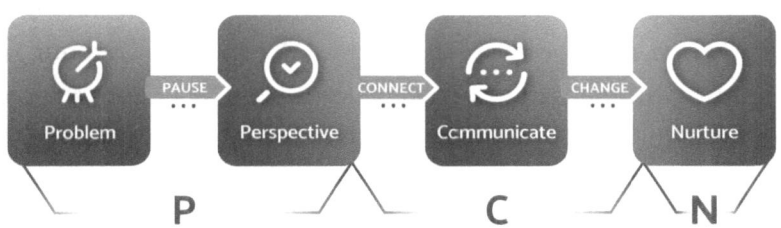

Let's explore how the PCN Method works in a common parenting scenario. Tina's sixteen-year-old daughter Lucy wants to attend her first concert without parental supervision.

Starting with Perspective (P)

When Lucy first asks about the concert, Tina notices her immediate internal reaction: anxiety, fear, and an urge to say, "Absolutely not!" But remembering her PCN training, she pauses to put on her logical lens. Instead of reacting from emotion, she opens with curiosity: "Tell me why you want to go to this concert."

Lucy shares her excitement about seeing her favorite band, spending time with friends, and feeling grown-up enough to handle this independence. Tina practices active listening and reflection: "I hear how important this is to you. The band means a lot to you, and you're feeling ready for more independence with your friends."

This perspective shift accomplishes two crucial things: it helps Tina understand Lucy's viewpoint, and it keeps Lucy's emotional brain calm enough to engage in problem-solving.

Moving to Communication (C)

Before diving into solutions, Tina acknowledges her own emotions using a "when, then, because" statement: "When you talk about going to a concert without parents, I feel nervous because I'm not sure you'll know what to do if a problem occurs. How can we come up with a plan that allows me to trust you so you can have fun with your friends?"

This honest communication opens the door for collaboration. Together, they explore various aspects of concert safety:

- transportation to and from the venue
- emergency contact plans
- meeting spots if friends get separated
- money for food and emergencies
- phone-charging solutions

When the discussion turns to timing, Tina sets a clear boundary: "I hear that you want to stay until the concert ends, but the last train home won't get you here until three a.m., and I am just not comfortable with that. Plus, we have a family event the next day. What might be a better solution for getting home earlier?" What might be a better solution for getting home on time?"

Though initially disappointed, Lucy engages in problem-solving. They agree on a midnight curfew, with Lucy's friend's older sister driving them home.

Nurturing through Consequences (**N**)

Now comes the crucial step of establishing consequences. Instead of imposing them, Tina asks: "What do you think should happen if you're not home by midnight?"

Lucy considers this carefully and suggests, "If I'm late, I lose your trust. I know you won't let me go to another concert again."

Mom agrees this is true but encourages a more immediate consequence to be discussed.

"I lose friend privileges for a week." This becomes their agreed-upon logical consequence—it's related to the situation, and, importantly, Lucy helped create it.

Tina confirms the agreement: "So we're clear, you'll be home by midnight. If you're on time, it shows me I can trust you with more independence in the future. If you're late, you're choosing to lose friend privileges for a week. Does that feel fair?"

This approach accomplishes several things:

◈ It respects Lucy's growing need for independence.
◈ It maintains clear boundaries for safety.
◈ It involves Lucy in creating solutions.
◈ It establishes clear, logical consequences.
◈ It provides motivation for making good choices.

The best part is that it begins to build on the trust both parent and child need to successfully help Lucy grow and develop within adolescence into a young adult.

Note: If Lucy returns on time, Tina will acknowledge this positive choice. More on rewards in the next chapter. But if Lucy is late, Tina will simply state, "I see you're choosing the consequence of no friend activities this week." Let's explore that more.

Pro tip: Consider the power of this simple statement. "I see YOU'RE choosing the consequence of...."

The moment when a child chooses not to follow through with an agreement often tempts parents into lengthy lectures or emotional responses. However, one simple phrase can transform these moments from power struggles into learning opportunities: "I see you're choosing the consequence of (insert agreed-upon consequence)."

This seemingly simple statement carries profound impact. When you say, "I see you're choosing the consequence of no TV tonight" instead of "That's it—you're losing TV privileges!" you

- acknowledge your child's agency in the decision
- remove yourself from the role of punisher
- eliminate the need for arguing or negotiating
- reinforce that this outcome was previously agreed upon
- place the responsibility squarely on your child's shoulders

Lisa, a parent in one of my workshops, initially doubted such a simple phrase could make a difference. "My son, Jake, always has a comeback for everything," she explained. But when she shifted from "You're grounded!" to "I see you're choosing the consequence of staying home this weekend" (a consequence they had previously agreed upon for breaking curfew), something changed. Jake paused, then replied, "I guess I did choose that, didn't I?"

The key here isn't just the words; it's the understanding that these consequences were revealed or agreed upon in advance. This isn't about surprising children with punishments; it's about respecting their ability to make choices while helping them learn from the outcomes.

However—and this is crucial—the effectiveness of this approach hinges entirely on what comes next: your follow-through. The most perfectly phrased consequence means nothing if you don't consistently enforce it!

The Power of Follow-Through

Enforcing consequences consistently isn't just about managing behavior; it's about teaching life lessons that extend far beyond childhood. As you learned in chapter 10, when parents follow through on agreed-upon consequences calmly and respectfully, they demonstrate integrity and build a foundation of trust that shapes their children's understanding of responsibility.

Consider Donna's experience with her nine-year-old daughter, Nicole. Every morning was a battle over getting ready for school on time, with Donna repeatedly threatening consequences but rarely following through. "Just five more minutes," Nicole would plead, and Donna would give in, rushing them both through a chaotic morning routine.

During a particularly stressful morning, Donna realized something had to change. The TV from the previous night had left Nicole too tired to wake up on time, making their morning routine even more challenging. She sat down with Nicole that evening, and together they created a clear agreement: if Nicole wasn't ready by seven thirty a.m., they agreed she would lose her evening TV time that day. The consequence was simple, related, and, most importantly, one that Donna knew she could consistently enforce.

The first morning Nicole tested the boundary, expecting the usual pattern of negotiations. Instead, Donna calmly stated, "I see you're choosing the consequence of skipping TV tonight by not being ready on time." Nicole protested, but Donna held firm. By the third morning, Nicole was ready at 7:25, and within two weeks, their morning struggles had virtually disappeared.

"The hardest part," Donna later shared, "wasn't coming up with the consequence; it was sticking to it that first time when she looked at me with those sad eyes. But now she trusts what I say because she knows I mean it. That trust is worth more than avoiding those few difficult moments."

This transformation illustrates why consistent follow-through matters: it turns empty words into meaningful life lessons, teaching children that their choices have real, predictable outcomes. Through this reliability, parents model the very responsibility they hope to instill, creating a legacy of accountability that serves children throughout their lives.

The Power of Positive Reinforcement

As we've explored in this chapter, effective consequences are not about control or suffering; they're about teaching children responsibility, accountability, and the real-life impact of their choices. By shifting from punishment to logical, agreed-upon consequences, you create a framework that supports learning, strengthens relationships, and nurtures growth.

But what about celebrating the wins? How do parents use positive reinforcement to encourage good behavior without creating a reliance on external rewards? In the next chapter, we'll dive into the art and science of rewards—how to use them effectively to motivate your children and reinforce the behaviors that bring harmony and joy to your home.

13

The Art of Effective Rewards – Creating Lasting Change

"If parents want to give their children a gift, the best thing they can do is to teach their children to love challenges, be intrigued by mistakes, enjoy effort, and keep on learning."

—Dr. Carol Dweck

When talking about "effective" rewards in parenting, it's not just about looking for what works today or tomorrow; it's about aiming for lasting behavioral change that shapes your child's future choices. This distinction is crucial because while many rewards might appear to work in the moment, research shows that different types of rewards create vastly different long-term outcomes.

Understanding Reward Types

While sticker charts and promised treats might drive short-term results, creating lasting behavioral change requires understanding of how different rewards impact children's internal motivation. Research shows that rewards can either foster dependency on external incentives or build genuine internal drive; the difference lies in how we implement them.

Consider two common scenarios I've witnessed in my practice. Ten-year-old Philip's parents offered him a new video game if he improved his grades. His studying increased dramatically—for about two weeks. Once he received the game, his motivation plummeted, and his parents found themselves searching for the next incentive.

In contrast, eight-year-old Jessica's parents took a different approach when addressing her academic challenges. They spent fifteen minutes each evening sharing "proud moments" from their day, including specific observations about Jessica's effort in schoolwork. Within months, Jessica had developed study habits that lasted throughout the school year, driven by her own sense of accomplishment and the meaningful connections she'd made with her parents.

As we explore deeper into effective rewards in this chapter, you'll discover how to move beyond quick fixes to create lasting positive changes. You'll learn why some rewards create temporary compliance while others build permanent internal motivation. Most importantly, you'll gain practical strategies for using rewards that don't just modify behavior today but help shape who your child becomes tomorrow.

The Science Behind Motivation

Every parent wants their child to feel motivated—not just to earn a reward, but because they genuinely care about what they're doing.

While offering treats or extra screen time can work in the short term, research shows that these material rewards often create a dependency on external incentives. Instead of developing a lasting internal drive, kids begin to ask, "What do I get for this?"

What truly fosters lasting change is helping children develop intrinsic motivation—the internal drive to engage in activities for their inherent enjoyment or personal satisfaction, not for external rewards. While material rewards like toys or gifts may spark quick action, the behavior may tend to fade once the reward disappears. Research from Ryan and Deci (2000) highlights that when children are engaged in activities that foster connection, like spending quality time together or participating in meaningful experiences—they build stronger, more enduring motivation. This helps them develop pride in mastering new skills, which increases intrinsic motivation and reinforces a sense of competence, self-direction, and emotional connection for the long term.

Think of it like teaching your child to ride a bike. Material rewards are like training wheels—helpful at first but not meant to last forever. Intrinsic rewards are the joy and confidence they feel when they ride on their own. By focusing on rewards that nurture connection and personal growth, you're helping your child develop the kind of motivation that lasts a lifetime.

Pick Your Hard: The Choice Between Short-Term Ease and Long-Term Growth

As a therapist, I often share this perspective with parents who feel stuck in cycles of quick fixes: "Let's talk about picking your hard." This usually earns me a puzzled look but stay with me.

Parenting presents us with two types of "hard." The first is the immediate challenge—dealing with tantrums, resistance to homework, bedtime battles, or morning routine struggles. It's tempting to reach for whatever will work right now: "Fine, you can have the iPad if you just get dressed!" Yes, this solves today's problem. But tomorrow? You're right back where you started, often with a child who now expects a reward for basic tasks.

The second type of "hard" is different. It's the challenging but transformative work of teaching internal motivation. It means weathering the storms of protest while you help your child develop their own reasons for positive choices. It's harder in the moment, absolutely. You might face more resistance initially. Your child might be upset. You might feel like the "mean parent" for a while.

But here's the crucial question I ask parents: "What would you rather have, immediate gratification with the same problem long-term or a short-term challenge that leads to lasting solutions?"

One mother's experience perfectly illustrates this choice. Cara struggled with her six-year-old's endless bedtime delays. She initially took the path of immediate gratification: negotiating, giving in to "just five more minutes," bribing with treats for tomorrow. Yes, it got her son to bed each night, but the cycle continued endlessly. When she chose the second "hard"—establishing and calmly maintaining a consistent bedtime routine without immediate rewards or negotiations—the first week was tough. Really tough. But by week three, her son was falling asleep independently, actually getting better rest, and showing up refreshed for school.

"Those first few nights were so hard," Cara shared, "but now I realize that what felt impossible for a week solved what had been impossible for a year."

This is what I mean by picking your hard. Both paths have their challenges, but only one leads to lasting change. The choice is yours; which hard would you prefer?

Nurturing the Seeds of Self-Motivation

Every child has an internal narrative: the stories they tell themselves about their abilities, efforts, and achievements. These self-narratives significantly impact motivation and resilience.

Jessa, a twelve-year-old client, demonstrated this powerful internal dialogue after completing a challenging puzzle: "I'm proud of myself for not giving up when it got hard." This moment exemplifies your goal—to have your children recognize and celebrate their own growth without depending on external motivators.

Growing these internal narratives requires intentional messaging from parents that shift focus from external to internal. When children learn to notice and value their own progress, they develop lasting intrinsic motivation.

Here are five ways parents can help nurture this development:

1. *Start with awareness questions.* Instead of immediately praising or rewarding, ask your child to notice their own experience. "How does it feel to have all your homework done before the weekend?" or "How does it feel to know you helped us with the kitchen cleanup tonight?"

2. *Encourage the process (reviewed in chapter 11).* Rather than general comments like "Good job!" or "You're the best!" highlight specific efforts and strategies. "I noticed you tried three different approaches before solving that science problem," or "You found a new way to organize your backpack; how did you think of that?"

3. *Create reflection opportunities.* Make it a family habit to share "proud moments" at dinnertime, focusing not just on achievements but on growth, effort, and problem-solving. Model this by sharing your own experiences: "I felt frustrated with a work

project today, but I'm proud that I took a break and came back with fresh ideas."

4. *Build natural rewards.* Link desired behaviors to meaningful privileges. "Once homework is complete, we'll have time for that game you love," or "When your room is organized, it'll be time for your favorite show."

5. *Foster independence.* Instead of jumping in with solutions, guide children to solve problems themselves. Help them set personal goals and create their own tracking systems. "What's your plan for finishing this project on time?" or "How will you know when you've reached your goal?"

When "Why" Isn't Enough: Teaching the "How"

Through years of working with families, I've discovered a crucial truth that often surprises parents: most children and teens actually understand why they shouldn't engage in certain behaviors, but many lack the practical skills to do things differently. But as you've learned, your role isn't to solve your kids' problems but to guide them in developing both the motivation and methods for sustainable change.

The strategies we've explored—from shifting rewards to building internal motivation—create the foundation for growth. However, implementing these approaches requires self-awareness and specific parenting skills. In the next chapter, you'll discover how your own self-awareness and growth can directly shape your child's development. When parents commit to understanding their own patterns and reactions, they create an environment where children can develop genuine confidence and capability.

14

Maintaining Your House Through Self-Awareness – When Parents Grow, Families Thrive

"The key to becoming a great parent is not better strategies but greater self-awareness."

—Dr. Shefali Tsabary

Twenty-two-year-old Brooke sat in our therapy session, a familiar place she'd been coming to since she was fifteen. "You know what's funny?" she said. "My mom is amazing in so many ways. She's supportive, open-minded, always there to talk . . . but the moment I'm upset about anything, it suddenly becomes about her feelings."

She shared a recent incident about a cherished decoration from her fish tank that her mother had accidentally thrown away. When Brooke expressed her disappointment, her mother's immediate response was, "So now I guess you're saying I'm a horrible mother?" What should have been a simple moment of acknowledging Brooke's feelings turned into Brooke having to console her mother instead.

This pattern had played out countless times over the years. Whether it was a disagreement about curfew, a discussion about college choices, or even simple daily frustrations, Brooke's emotions were consistently overshadowed by her mother's need for emotional reassurance. "I love my mom," Brooke explained, "but I've never really learned how to be upset around her. It's like my feelings are only okay if they don't make her feel bad about herself."

As we explored in chapter 5, parents naturally bring their own emotional baggage into their parenting journey—their past experiences, triggers, biases, and ingrained patterns of behavior. Brooke's mother, despite her many wonderful qualities, had a blind spot that prevented her from recognizing her role in their conflicts. Her own need for validation and reassurance often trumped her ability to simply hold space for her daughter's feelings.

This is where self-awareness becomes crucial in parenting. The more attuned parents are to their own emotional triggers and patterns, the better they can understand how these influences shape their reactions to their children. Self-awareness isn't just about recognizing your patterns; it's about acknowledging how these patterns impact your children's emotional development and their ability to form healthy relationships.

In this chapter, we'll explore three essential ways to use self-awareness to nurture and maintain the positive changes you've made through the PCN Method:

1. *Verbalizing Accountability*—learning to acknowledge your role in conflicts and miscommunications

2. *The Power of the Apology*—understanding how genuine apologies heal relationships and model emotional maturity

3. *"Can We Try Again?"*—embracing the opportunity to repair moments of disconnection and rebuild trust

These tools aren't just techniques; they're foundational skills that help parents maintain the healthy boundaries and connections they've worked so hard to establish. When parents commit to growing their self-awareness, they create space for their children to develop emotional intelligence and healthy relationship patterns that will serve them throughout their lives.

Verbalizing Accountability: "It's Me, Hi, I'm the Problem, It's Me"

Taylor Swift's viral lyrics capture a profound truth about relationships: sometimes we need to look in the mirror and acknowledge our own role in our struggles. This is especially true in parenting, where it's easy to fall into the trap of seeing our children as the sole source of family conflicts.

If you've been experiencing more struggles than smooth sailing with your kids, pause and consider: Do they believe that you think they're always the problem? And more importantly, do you? While children and teens certainly contribute to family challenges, relationships are a two-way street. The sooner you can acknowledge your part in conflicts, the sooner your child will feel safe enough to work on their part too.

Here's a truth that might be hard to hear. Like you learned in chapter 8, your child has no frame of reference for being older. Expecting them to meet you where you are emotionally is like expecting someone who's never seen a map to navigate cross-country. The good news is that you've been their age! Using your self-awareness to meet them where they are emotionally creates a massive bridge for understanding.

Let me share a personal story that illustrates this point. For years I nagged my family not to leave their shoes by the front door. Fun fact: my husband even promised in his wedding vows to me that he wouldn't leave his shoes lying around!

After redecorating our home, I thought we'd have a fresh start. When my oldest left her shoes by the door again, my emotions hijacked my reaction. The voices in my head screamed, *She doesn't care about my needs! She only cares about herself!* I exploded in anger, completely abandoning my PCN Method training.

But here's how self-awareness helped me gain perspective: while I was fixated on renovation costs and house maintenance, my daughter was simply excited to tell me about her day. For her, rushing in to share her stories mattered more than where her shoes landed. By letting my emotions override this understanding, I reacted with anger instead of connection, creating fear where I could have created learning. Any future compliance would come from that fear rather than understanding why the request mattered. And that would only weaken our relationship.

Two Ways to Take Accountability

1. Call It Like It Is

Instead of letting emotions push away the people you love most, it's essential to own your feelings in the moment. By "calling it like it is," you create emotional clarity that strengthens your connection with your child. Rather than yelling at your child for leaving shoes by the door, try saying, "I am feeling so frustrated about these shoes right now I want to yell." This simple shift does something powerful – it helps your child understand what's happening without making them responsible for managing your emotions.

While they did leave their shoes in the wrong place, owning your feelings allows them to see the situation clearly: the shoes need to be moved, and you're having a big feeling about it. This distinction is crucial. Your child learns that your emotions belong to you, not them.

Research shows that when parents openly acknowledge and verbalize their emotions, children develop stronger emotional competence and social skills by learning to understand their own and others' feelings (Green and Baker 2011). This emotional clarity also helps children realize they aren't responsible for their parents' feelings, which reduces confusion and anxiety—both crucial for building healthy relationships (Denham 2007).

2. Admit You Have a Problem

Sometimes the issue isn't just about feelings; it's about your own quirks and sensitivities. Take my experience with my eleven-year-old's love of Sephora body sprays. My heightened sensitivity to smells means her favorite scents give me instant headaches. Instead of attacking with, "Why would you put on so much? You know I hate strong odors!" I learned to say, "I know how much you love these scents, but my nose feels like it wants to explode. Could we find a way for you to enjoy your perfumes that works for both of us?"

Research in emotional regulation suggests that when parents model self-awareness and self-regulation, it helps children understand their own emotional responses and fosters more effective communication. This approach not only reduces conflict but strengthens the emotional connection between parent and child (Gottman, 1997).

The Transformative Power of Accountability

When parents verbalize self-awareness through accountability, they create a foundation for lasting positive change. This approach demonstrates mature problem-solving, strengthens parent-child bonds through humility and honesty, and empowers both parties to make changes. Most importantly, it prevents the resentment that grows when children feel constantly blamed for family problems.

> **Pro tip:** Before beginning the lessons you're learning from the PCN Method, consider opening a conversation with your kids by acknowledging your role in communication patterns.

"I've noticed our interactions aren't working as well as they could be, but I wanted you to know that I'm learning new ways to listen and respond. I might sound different as I practice these skills, and I know change can feel awkward, but I'm committed to doing this work because our relationship matters to me. We're in this together."

When kids see their parents actively working on growth, it not only feels like a huge dose of respect, but it is also a direct boost to their confidence. Most importantly, it transforms family dynamics from blame to partnership, creating an environment where both parent and child can acknowledge their growth areas without fear of judgment.

Accountability isn't about being perfect; it's about being honest. When parents model this vulnerability about their own struggles and growth, they create space for children to do the same.

As one teen client shared, "When my mom started admitting she was wrong at times too, I felt less defensive and more open to hearing her side of the story." This authentic sharing creates new possibilities for deeper understanding and connection, allowing families to navigate challenges together rather than against each other.

The Power of the Apology: When "I'm Sorry" Changes Everything

Sixteen-year-old Danny sat in my office, tears welling in his eyes as he described a fight with his father. "He yelled at me in front of my friends about leaving my bike in the rain. I get that I made a mistake, but it was an honest accident. I don't see why he couldn't just talk to me about it away from my friends. And what hurts most is that when I asked for an apology, he said he didn't owe me anything and went on to just act like it never happened."

This moment crystallized something I've observed repeatedly in my practice: the profound impact of parental apologies—or their absence.

Danny wasn't trying to avoid taking responsibility for leaving his bike out in the rain. He was just asking his dad to acknowledge how his yelling made him feel in front of his friends.

The simple act of saying "I'm sorry" carries extraordinary power in the parent-child relationship. Research by Oostenbroek and Vaish (2019) found that parental apologies serve as crucial teaching moments that help children develop their own moral compass. Yet many parents often hesitate to apologize to their children, fearing it may undermine their authority. This reluctance creates a paradox, as parents expect their children to apologize when they're wrong but may struggle to model this behavior themselves.

Consider what happened with Becky and her thirteen-year-old daughter, Sam. After snapping at Sam during a stressful morning rush, Becky had a choice. Had she followed her initial instinct to justify her behavior—"Well, if you had been ready on time . . ."—the morning could have spiraled into mutual resentment.

Instead, Becky caught herself and said, "I'm sorry for yelling. I was stressed about being late, but that's not an excuse for speaking to you that way." Sam's response was immediate and touching: "Thanks, Mom. I know mornings are hard for both of us." When Becky acknowledged her specific behavior, took responsibility without excuses, and showed understanding of the impact, she not only repaired the moment but allowed them both to get through the morning rush without any unnecessary added conflict.

The Art of Forgiveness: A Message for Your Perspective

As previously discussed, parents often hesitate to apologize to their children fearing it might undermine their authority. Rather than think of apologizing as something "bad," think about it as though you are teaching your children one of life's most valuable skills: the art of forgiveness.

Consider thirteen-year-old Josephine's reflection: "When my mom apologizes for overreacting, it helps me understand that everyone has hard days. It makes me feel better knowing she is just human, just like me, and she can make mistakes too."

When parents apologize authentically, they model how forgiveness strengthens relationships and fosters growth. One father shared how his apology transformed a conflict with his son about a broken gaming controller. Instead of demanding immediate repayment, he apologized for his harsh reaction and opened a discussion about responsibility and accidents. "I watched my son's whole demeanor change," he noted. "He went from defensive to solutions focused.

Now when things go wrong, he comes to me right away because he knows we'll handle it together."

Think of it this way: every time you apologize sincerely, you're not just fixing a moment; you're building your child's emotional tool kit for all their future relationships. You're showing them that strong people can admit mistakes, that relationships are worth the work of repair, and that growth comes from how we handle our missteps, not from being perfect.

"Can We Try Again?": Creating Space for Growth and Connection

The simple phrase "Can we try again?" developed by Howard Glasser in his Nurtured Heart Approach, holds remarkable power to transform mistakes into opportunities for connection and growth. This technique provides children with a chance to correct their behavior without shame or punishment (Glasser 2002).

I witnessed this with the Martinez family, where fourteen-year-old Ana and her mother were locked in constant arguments about housework. During one heated session, Ana's mother paused mid-lecture and said, "I'm not handling this well. Can we try again?" The tension dissolved immediately, leading to their first genuine conversation in weeks about Ana's struggles with responsibilities.

A "try again" goes beyond a simple apology—it demonstrates an active commitment to improvement. When parents use this approach, they show their children that growth is possible and relationships matter more than being right. One father shared, "At first, it felt weird, like admitting weakness. But then my son started using it too. When he snapped at his sister, he stopped himself: 'Wait, can I try that again?' I realized I was teaching him relationship repair."

This practice connects directly to the PCN Method by allowing parents to return to the perspective phase. Like editing a story, it offers a chance to revise our approach with fresh eyes. When children see parents using try agains, they learn that mistakes are opportunities for growth, and that taking a pause is a strength rather than weakness.

One mother transformed daily conflicts over food wrappers through this approach. Instead of launching into her usual lecture about cleanliness, she said, "I'm getting upset about these wrappers. Would you like a try again with how we handle snacks?" Her daughter, Catie, visibly relaxed and suggested creating a better system together. This became their pattern, with Catie eventually using it proactively: "Mom, before you get upset about the wrapper under my desk, can we try again? I have an idea." As her mother reflected, "It's like a pause button. We're not fighting about wrappers anymore. We're building better habits together."

Building Your Self-Awareness Practice

Just as a well-maintained house requires regular care, nurturing your parental self-awareness demands consistent attention and thoughtful upkeep. Think of it like maintaining different areas of your home: some tasks need daily attention, others require weekly check-ins, and some call for monthly deep dives.

Your daily maintenance might look like a quick emotional inventory each morning, similar to checking that all the lights work and the doors are secure. Take a moment to check in with yourself: How are you feeling? What energy are you bringing to the day? Throughout the day, build in brief pauses before responding to challenges; these are like the small adjustments you make to keep your house running smoothly. End each day with a few minutes of reflection on your parenting moments, just as you might straighten up the living room before bed.

Weekly tune-ups involve deeper work. Set aside time to review challenging interactions for patterns, much like checking your home's systems for potential issues. Did you notice yourself getting triggered in similar situations? Were there moments when you successfully used your PCN skills? Celebrate these victories and learning moments—they're like fixing a squeaky door or finally organizing that messy drawer. Use these observations to plan adjustments for the coming week.

Monthly renovations require more substantial reflection. Just as you might tackle bigger home improvement projects monthly, schedule time for deeper parenting work. Evaluate your parenting goals: Are your boundaries still serving their purpose? How has your family grown and changed? Celebrate the progress you've made together—perhaps your try agains are becoming more natural or your apologies more genuine. These moments of growth are like successful renovation projects that make your home more comfortable and functional.

Your journey of self-awareness will have its messy moments. The goal is never about perfection but progress and to create an emotional environment where your family can thrive, grow, and feel secure together.

Building on Your Foundation

When parents commit to self-awareness through accountability, apologies, and try agains, they create what psychologists call a "secure emotional environment"—a space where both parents and children feel safe to grow, make mistakes, and learn together. Research rooted in attachment theory suggests that children thrive when they feel emotionally secure, as it provides a stable foundation for exploration, learning, and healthy relationships (Ainsworth et al., 1978). Like a well-maintained house, these practices require consistent attention and care, but the rewards are immeasurable: stronger relationships, better communication, and a family culture built on trust and understanding.

As we move into the next chapter, you'll discover four natural ways to nurture your PCN progress: the power of hugs, the gift of shared laughter, the bond of exercising together, and the impact of scheduled quality time. These simple but powerful tools will help strengthen the positive changes you've already made within your family.

Just as a house needs more than just maintenance to feel like a home, your relationship with your children needs more than just repairs; it needs moments of joy, laughter, and shared celebration. These tools will help you create an atmosphere where your new skills can flourish and your family bonds can continue to strengthen.

15

Natural Ways to Nurture Your New Connection

"Parents are the ultimate role models for children. Every word, every movement, and action affects. No other person or outside force has a greater influence on a child than the parent."

—Bob Keeshan (*Captain Kangaroo*)

Building new patterns with your children through the PCN Method is like renovating a house—the major work may be complete, but now comes the joy of making that house truly feel like a home. Just as a newly renovated space needs warmth and personal touches to feel lived in, your refreshed relationship with your children needs natural, ongoing nurturing to fully thrive.

In this chapter, you'll discover four powerful, scientifically proven ways to strengthen your family bonds: the healing power of physical affection, the connecting force of shared laughter, the bonding effect of moving together, and the deepening impact of dedicated time. These aren't just feel-good suggestions; they're essential tools that work with your brain's chemistry to reinforce the positive changes you've already made.

Think of these approaches as the finishing touches on your family renovation project. While the PCN Method has given you the framework for healthy interactions, these natural nurturing techniques add the warmth and connection that make your relationship changes lasting and meaningful. Just as you might add family photos and comfortable furnishings to make a house feel like home, these strategies help transform your improved communication patterns into deep, lasting family bonds.

The Power of Touch: Building Bridges Through Physical Connection

In their study of emotional intelligence in *The Whole-Brain Child*, Dr. Daniel Siegel and Tina Payne Bryson (2011) illustrate the profound power of nonverbal communication in parent-child relationships. During moments of emotional intensity, gestures like a compassionate hug or an empathetic facial expression can speak more loudly than words. These nonverbal connections can help foster emotional regulation and create deeper understanding between parents and children, serving as essential tools for nurturing emotional development.

The science of physical touch also highlights what a powerful role it plays in human connection. Research suggests that even a brief hug, lasting around twenty seconds, can trigger significant physiological benefits for both parent and child. During physical contact, bodies naturally synchronize—heart rates slow, breathing patterns align, and stress levels decrease—promoting a sense of calm and emotional bonding (Field 2001).

Additionally, when parents hug or share loving touch, bodies release oxytocin, often called the "bonding hormone." This powerful chemical creates what neuroscientists describe as a neurochemical bridge between parent and child. This biological dance creates an environment where connection can flourish and conflicts are less likely to escalate.

But what happens when traditional hugs become challenging, as they often do with teenagers? This was the question facing Amanda, mother of fifteen-year-old Lexi. As her daughter entered adolescence, the easy physical affection of childhood disappeared. "It felt like there was this physical wall between us," Amanda shared during a therapy session. "Lexi would actually flinch if I tried to hug her, and it was breaking my heart."

The breakthrough came when Amanda remembered something from Lexi's childhood: her daughter had always loved foot rubs while watching TV. "I casually offered one evening while we were watching her favorite show," Amanda recalled. "Her whole face lit up." This became their new ritual: weekly foot rubs during their shared TV time. Through this simple form of touch, they found a way to maintain physical connection that felt comfortable and natural for both of them.

The impact went far beyond those quiet evening moments. Amanda noticed that on days following their foot rub sessions, Lexi was more open to conversation, less defensive, and more likely to share details about her life. "It's like that physical connection opens up other channels of communication," Amanda observed. Even more surprisingly, Lexi started initiating other forms of physical affection—a quick shoulder squeeze while passing in the kitchen or leaning against her mom while looking at photos on her phone.

Any form of loving touch, whether it's a hug, a foot rub, or a gentle pat on the shoulder, activates our neural reward centers. Even for teenagers, who are biologically wired to seek independence while still needing security, finding comfortable ways to maintain physical connection can create a crucial bridge during these years. These moments of connection release chemicals that make us feel safe, understood, and bonded.

The Healing Power of Humor: When Laughter Bridges Divides

The transformative power of laughter in family dynamics cannot be overstated. According to a study by Dr. Robert Provine (2000), a neuroscientist who specializes in the science of laughter, humor can help reduce stress, foster cooperation, and even strengthen family relationships by promoting positive emotional connections. In this way laughter acts as a social glue, allowing families to recover more quickly from disagreements and navigate life's challenges with greater ease.

Consider what happens in your body when you laugh. Your brain releases endorphins, nature's feel-good chemicals, creating positive associations with family interactions. These moments of shared joy don't just feel good; they actually rewire brains to approach future interactions with more optimism and flexibility. When a parent and child laugh together, they create a shared experience that builds family identity and often evolves into cherished inside jokes.

Nora discovered this power accidentally one afternoon when her twelve-year-old son, Ryan, once again forgot to empty his lunch box after school. Having reminded him countless times, she felt the familiar frustration rising. But instead of launching into her usual lecture, something sparked a different response. Walking into the kitchen where the days-old lunch box sat, she dramatically clutched her chest, staggered backward, and declared in her best theatrical voice, "Oh, the smell! I've been poisoned by the toxic waste of forgotten sandwiches!"

Ryan, expecting the usual scolding, froze for a moment before bursting into laughter. "Mom, you're so weird," he giggled, then promptly moved to clean out the offensive lunch box. What could have been another tense moment of parent-child conflict transformed into a shared laugh that actually accomplished the desired goal.

"It became our thing," Nora shared. "Now whenever something's been forgotten—homework, chores, whatever—one of us will do the dramatic faint routine. It completely shifts the energy. Instead of me being the nagging mom and him being the forgetful kid, we're just two people sharing a silly moment."

When parents approach challenges with playfulness, they demonstrate emotional flexibility while creating opportunities for trust. Humor breaks down defenses, making both parties more open to problem-solving. Each lighthearted moment builds family resilience, transforming potential conflicts into opportunities for connection.

Movement as Connection: The Exercise Effect

Engaging in shared physical activities can enhance mood and health by promoting the release of endorphins and reducing stress hormones like cortisol, thereby fostering better connection and communication among individuals. Regular exercise has also been shown to improve mood, reduce stress, and enhance overall well-being.

Linda, mother of ten-year-old Jackson, knows this struggle intimately. "I'm what you'd call a professional couch potato," she laughed during one of our sessions. "My ideal afternoon involves blankets, books, and absolutely zero movement. But Jackson? He's like a perpetual motion machine."

The mismatch in their energy levels created genuine challenges. While Linda craved quiet downtime, Jackson literally bounced off walls with pent-up energy, leading to increased conflicts and frustration on both sides. Everything changed when Linda made a commitment to step out of her comfort zone and into Jackson's world of movement.

"I started small," she explained. "We'd do fifteen-minute walks after dinner. I won't lie—some days I had to practically drag myself out the door. But I noticed something interesting: no matter how reluctant I felt at the start, I always came back feeling more patient, more connected to Jackson, and somehow more energized."

Their walks gradually extended into neighborhood explorations, playground visits, and even occasional jog-walk combinations. The most surprising discovery? "After we've had our active time together, Jackson is actually ready for those cozy moments I love. It's like he needed to burn off his physical energy before he could settle into emotional connection. Now we get the best of both worlds—adventure and snuggles."

Research also shows that physical movement can significantly improve communication among family members by reducing the pressure of direct, face-to-face conversations (Gottman 1999). I witnessed this phenomenon firsthand with my own daughters on a cold winter morning. No one wanted to attempt the hiking trail I'd suggested, myself included. The complaints were numerous: "It's too cold!" "I'm tired!" "Can't we just stay home?" But something told me to persist gently.

Two hours later we found ourselves at the summit of a local trail, cheeks flushed from effort and eyes bright with accomplishment. The transformation was remarkable. My typically reserved tweenager openly shared stories about school challenges. My older daughter, often normally glued to her device, pointed out interesting plants and rocks. That evening, when I asked about their favorite part of the day, they unanimously declared, "The hike we didn't want to take!"

Whether hiking, playing sports, or simply walking together, shared movement creates lasting memories and strengthens family bonds, building resilience for challenging times.

Beyond Daily Routines: The Power of Scheduled Connection

The time parents spend with their children can be divided into incidental, day-to-day interactions and deliberately scheduled one-on-one time. While both are important, experts emphasize that consciously investing quality, undivided attention sends a powerful message of love and worth to a child.

Intentional, dedicated time with children communicates their importance. When a parent intentionally sets aside time specifically for them—marking it in a calendar, protecting it from interruptions—children receive a powerful message: *I am a priority in my parent's life*. Research indicates that the time parents spend with their children significantly influences the children's well-being. Research also shows that the quality of time parents spend with their children, not just the quantity, positively impacts child well-being and development (Cano et al. 2018; Milkie et al. 2015). Consider fourteen-year-old Diana's experience. Her mother, a busy executive, started blocking out two hours every Sunday afternoon for what they called "Diana Time." No phones, no siblings, no agenda—just dedicated space for whatever Diana wanted to do together. "The first few weeks felt awkward," her mother admitted. "We were both so used to multitasking our conversations between other activities. But something shifted when Diana realized this time was truly hers—that I wouldn't suddenly need to answer an email or help her brother with homework."

The neuroscience of anticipation and reward is fascinating. Research on dopamine reveals how the brain's reward system responds to anticipated experiences, releasing the neurotransmitter associated with motivation and pleasure (Volkow et al. 2011). This can then create a "positive feedback loop," where a parent's positive attention can increase a child's cooperative behavior and strengthen the parent-child relationship.

Even more compelling is how scheduled time affects behavior outside these special moments. Seven-year-old Brandon's father noticed a significant change in their daily interactions after designating ten minutes of one-on-one reading time before getting ready for the day. The guaranteed time together seemed to reduce Brandon's attention-seeking behaviors after school, he observed. "It's like giving him that extra special time helped him feel secure enough to be more independent throughout the day."

This makes sense from a psychological perspective. When children don't have to compete for a parent's attention or wonder when they'll next have meaningful connection, they're free to focus on healthy development rather than seeking attention through potentially disruptive behaviors. The security of scheduled time creates an emotional anchor that stabilizes the entire parent-child relationship.

From Conscious Effort to Natural Connection

As we've explored in this chapter, nurturing your PCN progress through physical touch, laughter, movement, and scheduled quality time isn't just about adding pleasant activities to your day; it's about creating the conditions for lasting transformation in your family dynamics. These natural forms of connection work with your brain's chemistry to reinforce the positive changes you've already made through the PCN Method.

Think of it like tending a garden. The PCN Method helped you prepare the soil and plant the seeds of change. Now these nurturing practices—from a well-timed hug to a shared laugh, from a spontaneous hike to a scheduled "just us" afternoon—are like the sunlight and water that help your garden flourish. Each positive interaction strengthens the roots of your connection, making your relationship more resilient and your new patterns more natural.

In the next chapter, we'll delve into the fascinating neuroscience behind these changes. You'll discover how each time you choose the PCN Method over "fix-it mode" solutions, you're not just making a conscious choice; you're actually rewiring your brain. We'll explore exactly how these new patterns of interaction create new neural pathways, gradually transforming what once felt like difficult conscious efforts into natural, automatic responses.

Just as your old patterns took time to develop, these new ways of connecting with your children need time and consistent practice to become your new normal. But with each day, each interaction, and each moment of intentional connection, you're building something remarkable: a stronger, more resilient, more joyful relationship with your child.

16

The Science of Change – How the PCN Method Rewires Your Brain

"The brain is wider than the sky."

—Emily Dickinson

While you're actively nurturing all these new changes in your relationship with your child, something remarkable is happening inside your brain. Scientists call it neuroplasticity—your brain's extraordinary ability to reorganize itself by forming new neural connections. Think of it like creating new pathways through an overgrown field; the more you walk the same path, the clearer and easier to follow it becomes.

Siegel and Bryson's (2011) research on neuroplasticity reveals how our brains are not fixed, but malleable. Through the PCN Method, parents can fundamentally reshape their communication patterns.

Just as a well-trodden path becomes smooth and natural, repeated intentional interactions gradually transform conscious efforts into automatic, more intuitive responses. This means communication strategies don't just improve immediate interactions; they create lasting neurological changes that fundamentally alter how parents and children connect.

Consider Maria's experience with her fourteen-year-old son. "At first," she shared, "stopping to consider his perspective when he was pushing my buttons felt almost impossible. It was like trying to speak a foreign language. But after a few months of practicing the PCN Method, I found myself naturally pausing before reacting. One day my son even commented, 'Mom, you're different now. You actually listen before getting upset.'"

Research on neuroplasticity further supports this idea. Dr. Norman Doidge's groundbreaking work reveals how the brain possesses a remarkable ability to reshape itself through repeated experiences (Doidge 2007). This means that intentional, repeated actions can literally rewire the brain, creating more efficient neural connections and transforming how we think, learn, and interact.

This has profound implications for parenting each time you

◈ pause to consider your child's perspective
◈ choose communication that focuses on connection over correction
◈ reinforce changes through nurture

You're not just handling a single interaction differently; you're literally rebuilding your brain's response patterns, making it easier to connect and communicate with your child. The following section provides practical tips to help parents recognize their brain's transformation through the PCN Method.

The "Wait, I Handled That Differently!" Moment

Pay attention to those surprising moments when you naturally respond in a new way without having to think about it. These "automatic" PCN responses are your brain's way of showing you that new neural pathways are forming. For example, you might find yourself

◈ automatically pausing before reacting to a situation that would have triggered an immediate emotional response before

◈ naturally considering your child's perspective without having to remind yourself

◈ catching yourself using PCN language without conscious effort

◈ feeling calmer in situations that previously caused intense reactions

When you notice these moments, celebrate them! They're concrete evidence that your brain is literally rewiring itself. Think of them as "neural notifications"—your brain's way of telling you, *Hey, we're creating a new default setting here!*

One mother described her realization perfectly: "I knew something had changed when my daughter said something sassy and instead of immediately jumping in to lecture her, I found myself thinking, *Did she mean to say it that way? Is she upset about something or someone? Let me ask her first before automatically assuming.* It wasn't a conscious choice; it just happened. That's when I realized the PCN Method wasn't just something I was doing anymore; it was becoming who I am."

Tracking Your Parenting Neural Changes: A Simple Guide

Discovering how your brain is rewiring itself can be both exciting and transformative. Here are three straightforward ways to notice and celebrate the positive changes in your parenting approach.

1. Phone Tracking: Your Digital Parenting Notebook

Think of your smartphone as a personal growth companion. When you notice a moment where you respond differently, take a quick note. For example, imagine catching yourself moving from "fix-it mode" to a more compassionate approach. Jot down what happened: "Old me would have immediately tried to solve my child's problem. Today I listened and reflected back what they were feeling." Think about how this new response made you feel. Was there a sense of calm? Did you notice less tension in your body? And what was the outcome as a result? More fighting and disconnect? Or more connection and problem-solving? These small moments are powerful indicators of your brain creating new neural pathways.

2. Visual Connection: Using CBT Circles for Perspective Shifts

One effective way to track your progress is by mapping your thinking patterns using three interconnected circles, building on the Cognitive Behavioral Therapy (CBT) Circle Chart you first saw in chapter 3.

Start by documenting your first thought about a challenging situation in circle 1. Remember, this is the immediate mental interpretation that springs to mind. Then, explore how that thought triggers an emotional response in circle 2. Notice how the thought directly creates a specific feeling. Finally, in circle 3, describe the behavior that emerges from that emotional state.

For example . . .

Original Emotional Response:

◈ Thought circle: *He's deliberately ignoring me.*

◈ Feeling circle: Frustrated and disrespected

◈ Behavior circle: Raised voice, demanded attention

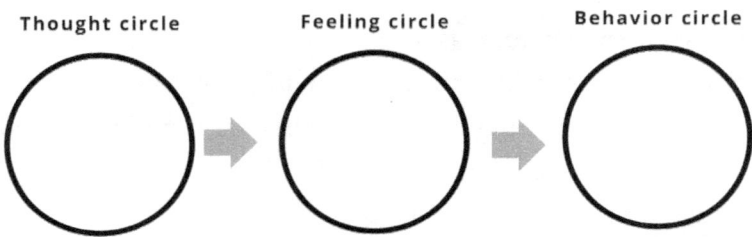

Using the next three circles, re-frame your narrative using your new perspective tools. How are you thinking about the situation differently? How do these different thoughts (circle 1) lead to different feelings (circle 2) and actions (circle 3)?

For example . . .

Reframed Logical Response:

◈ Thought circle: *He might be absorbed in his activity.*

◈ Feeling circle: Curious and patient

◈ Behavior circle: Approached calmly, waited for natural pause

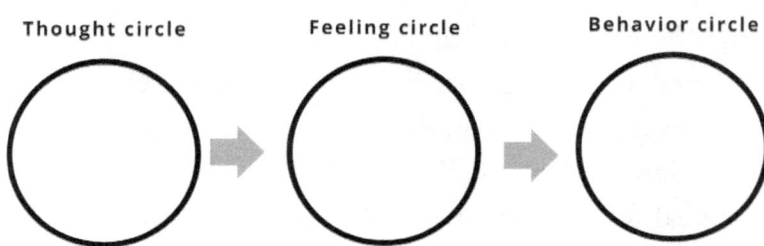

This visual comparison helps make abstract brain changes tangible, showing how perspective shifts create real changes in your parenting responses.

3. Family Feedback: Your Loved Ones as Mirrors

Your family can be your most honest observers. Regularly ask them, "How am I showing up differently?" Children and partners often notice changes before we do. They might share observations like, "You seem more patient," or "I noticed you listened without getting upset." These external perspectives can be incredibly validating and provide additional insight into your personal growth.

Remember, the magic is in the consistency and compassion you bring to this process. You're not just changing behaviors; you're reshaping your brain's default settings. Each small moment of awareness is a celebration, a neural notification that you're becoming the parent you've always wanted to be. Some days will be easier than others, and that's okay. The fact that you're paying attention and trying is what matters most.

17

Finding the Sweet Spot – Why the PCN Method Is NOT the Same as Other Gentle Parenting Strategies

"Parenting is a constant balancing act. It's about guiding, not controlling; teaching, not lecturing; and encouraging, not demanding."

—Anonymous

Parents often express valid skepticism about "gentle parenting" approaches. "If I'm not strict, my kids will walk all over me," they worry. Or "I tried being gentle, but my kids stopped listening altogether." These concerns are valid and stem from a common misconception: that gentle parenting doesn't work. Let's clear up this crucial distinction and understand why the PCN Method offers a more balanced and effective approach.

The Gentle Parenting Trap

Gentle parenting typically emerges from good intentions—parents wanting to avoid the harsh disciplinary methods they may have experienced in their own childhood. However, when a parent doesn't discipline with limits, their parenting can become too permissive. If you remember from chapter 5, being too permissive often swings too far in the opposite direction, creating its own set of problems. In permissive households, parents might avoid setting clear boundaries for fear of upsetting their children, give in to demands to prevent tantrums, or struggle to maintain consistent consequences.

The result? Children who feel increasingly emotionally unsafe and unsure, despite (or perhaps because of) their apparent "freedom."

 Remember: Without clear boundaries and guidance, children miss out on crucial learning opportunities and the security that comes from knowing their parents can handle difficult situations. This uncertainty often manifests as increased anxiety, testing behaviors, and power struggles—the very outcomes parents were trying to avoid.

The Strict Parenting Problem

Traditional strict parenting often stems from fear—parents worried their children won't develop discipline or respect without some type of rigid control at home. However, when parents rely too heavily on punishment and authority, they create a different set of long-term challenges. In chapter 5, you learned that authoritarian parents (the

"Director" type) might enforce rules without explanation, use threats or punishment as primary motivators, or struggle to maintain emotional connection while asserting control.

The result? Children who comply out of fear rather than understanding. While strict parenting might appear effective on the surface—achieving immediate obedience—it often leads to decreased self-esteem, suppressed communication, and damaged trust. Children learn to hide their mistakes instead of seeking guidance, develop anxiety about making decisions, or rebel dramatically once they gain independence. Most concerningly, they miss opportunities to develop internal motivation, instead learning to act based on external control.

Why the PCN Method Works Differently

Unlike traditional parenting approaches that fall into extremes—either overly permissive or strictly authoritarian—the PCN Method builds on three fundamental human needs: connection through perspective and understanding, self-determination through guided collaboration and choices, and safety through consistent strategic nurturing. By addressing these core needs in a specific sequence, the method develops conflict resolution skills that serve children throughout their lives, from playground disputes to future career decisions.

The journey begins with perspective—creating emotional safety through regulated, empathetic responses. Instead of reacting to emotions without direction, parents establish themselves as emotional anchors. By remaining regulated and understanding children's viewpoints, you demonstrate strong leadership while making them feel truly seen before any problem-solving begins.

Next, communication builds self-determination through structured choices and collaboration. Rather than allowing unlimited negotiations or enforcing rigid control, the PCN Method guides children to contribute within clear boundaries. For example, instead of open-ended bedtime discussions, a parent might say, "Would you like to start your routine with a bath or with pajamas?" This maintains parental leadership while developing internal motivation and problem-solving skills.

Finally, nurturing establishes safety through consistent, connection-based consequences. Unlike permissive approaches that may avoid boundaries or strict methods that can damage trust, the PCN Method requires clear limits delivered with empathy. This creates the emotional safety children need to develop self-discipline and positive cooperation.

These components must work together; focusing on just one or two creates imbalance. Consider ten-year-old Izzy refusing to clean up after dinner.

A fragmented approach might

- use perspective without action ("I understand you have big feelings about cleaning up") but never solve the problem.
- communicate choices without limits ("What do you want to do instead?") which can invite inappropriate options.
- set boundaries without connection ("No playdates this entire weekend if you can't follow through with your chores") which triggers resistance.

The PCN Method integrates all three.

1. Perspective: "It looks like you're not in the mood to clean up after dinner. I know cleaning up isn't fun especially when you're extra tired."
2. Communication: "Clean up needs to be completed before screen time. What seems easiest to clean up first? Do you need help coming up with ideas to break it into smaller chunks?"

3. Nurture: "You're doing an awesome job cleaning up. Doesn't it feel good to help? I know how tired you were, so thank you!"

When these components work together, children develop lasting behavioral change. They make better choices not from fear or lack of limits but from genuine understanding and motivation. This creates confident, resilient children who trust their parents' guidance while developing their own internal compass.

Why All Three Components Matter

 Remember: The PCN Method positions parents as guides who teach, support, and maintain boundaries while honoring their children's developmental needs for connection, self-determination, and safety. This balanced approach helps children develop internal motivation and self-discipline, rather than either external compliance or unchecked impulses.

The Parent as Guide

When parents consistently apply all three components of the PCN Method, they create an environment where children feel secure enough to learn from their mistakes, capable enough to participate in problem-solving, and supported enough to handle life's challenges. This isn't gentle parenting; it's purposeful parenting that builds lasting skills and stronger relationships.

Why Good Intentions Don't Always Lead to Good Results

You've gotten this far, and you are clearly committed to being more purposeful and collaborative. Yet somehow your attempts at the PCN Method aren't working the way you want them to. Your children might be pushing back harder or becoming increasingly dependent on you for solutions. Maybe you're left wondering, *Where did I go wrong?*

Remember These Common Pitfalls in PCN Method Parenting Attempts

1. *The Rush to Rescue (aka Fix-It Mode):* Francesca thought she was doing everything right with her thirteen-year-old son, Brian. When he struggled with math, she immediately offered solutions: "Why don't we get a tutor?" "How about I help you study?" "Let's make flash cards!" But the more solutions she offered, the more Brian withdrew. During a therapy session, Brian revealed, "Mom never gives me a chance to figure things out. It's like she doesn't trust me to solve my own problems."

 Remember: This common pattern—rushing to rescue—albeit with good intentions, actually undermines a child's developing right to self-determination. When parents jump straight to solutions, they unintentionally send the message, "I don't trust you to handle this." Over time, children either stop sharing their struggles (why bother when Mom or Dad will

just take over?) or become dependent on their parents for every decision.

2. *The Emotion Overflow.* Consider Louisa, who prided herself on being emotionally attuned to her children. When her nine-year-old daughter mentioned struggling with friendship issues at school, Louisa immediately responded with overwhelming concern: "Oh no, that's terrible! I'm so worried about you not having friends. Are you being excluded? Do we need to talk to the teacher? Should I call the other parents?" While her worry came from a place of love, Louisa's daughter eventually stopped confiding in her because managing her mother's anxiety became overwhelming. Children often become emotional caretakers when parents share their own worries and fears before establishing a foundation of perspective through validation and understanding. There is a place for expressing appropriate concern after your child feels connected through perspective.

3. *The Choice Overload.* Consider Steve, who thought he was empowering his six-year-old by offering unlimited breakfast options. "Do you want a smoothie, pancakes, waffles, cereal, or eggs? If you want cereal, which of these seven boxes? Do you want milk? Almond milk? Oat milk?" Even while his daughter was eating her chosen cereal, Steve continued, "Do you want fruit with that? Banana? Strawberries? Or maybe you'd rather have toast now?" But too many open-ended choices without clear boundaries created anxiety rather than autonomy. His daughter began showing signs of stress at mealtimes, sometimes even refusing to eat breakfast altogether as the barrage of options became overwhelming. Rather than feeling empowered, she felt burdened by the constant

decision-making and her inability to satisfy her father's enthusiasm for her "independence."

4. *The Conditional Connection.* Dani tried implementing the PCN Method techniques, but only when her children's behavior didn't trigger her emotionally. Instead, during conflicts, she reverted to punishment and control. This inconsistency left her kids confused about what to expect, creating a pattern where they only felt safe sharing positive experiences—hiding their struggles and mistakes when they needed guidance most.

 Remember: The PCN Method isn't about parental perfection; it's about being purposeful and present. Every interaction becomes an opportunity to strengthen the parent-child bond, foster independence, and build a lasting trust that goes far deeper than surface-level compliance. As children feel truly understood—not just loved but comprehensively seen—they develop an internal compass that guides them toward better choices and healthier relationships.

Frequently Asked Questions: Navigating the PCN Method

Question: "Will my child really go for this?"

Your child's resistance isn't a rejection of connection; it's a protective mechanism carefully constructed over years of previous interactions. Think of it like a fortress they've built to keep themselves emotionally safe. If you're doubting your child will go for these changes, what you're really describing is a child who has learned to protect themselves from vulnerability.

This protective wall didn't appear overnight. It's the result of years of experiences where they might have felt

- ◈ rushed when trying to express themselves
- ◈ dismissed when sharing difficult emotions
- ◈ solved for, instead of supported
- ◈ criticized for their struggles
- ◈ punished for showing vulnerability

Maybe you've been the parent who

- ◈ jumps in to fix problems before your child can process them
- ◈ offers solutions instead of listening
- ◈ becomes frustrated when they don't immediately cooperate
- ◈ uses fear or punishment as a primary motivator
- ◈ inadvertently sends the message that their feelings are inconvenient

The PCN Method works precisely because it dismantles these old patterns systematically. It's not about a quick fix but about rebuilding trust through consistent, compassionate interactions. The PCN Method doesn't demand they tear down their protective walls immediately. Instead, it gently shows them that the space beyond the wall is safe. You're not trying to break through; you're inviting them to explore a different way of connecting.

Note: This approach requires patience. Your child may test you, expecting the old patterns. They might

- ◈ withdraw when you try to connect
- ◈ comply at first but then fall back into old patterns

- ◈ challenge your new approach
- ◈ seem skeptical of your changed interactions

These are actually positive signs. Your child is carefully checking: *Is this real? Can I trust this new way of being?*

The transformation happens slowly, then all at once. One day you'll realize they're sharing something vulnerable. They'll look up, waiting for the old reaction—and instead, they'll find understanding. That's when the wall starts to crumble.

Question: "Is physical intervention ever okay in PCN parenting?"

They key to remember is that physical intervention is about protection, not control. There are rare, critical moments when physical intervention isn't just acceptable—it's absolutely necessary to protect your child's life and safety. The key is understanding the difference between physical intervention for safety and physical punishment.

To help you know the distinction, think of the Potato Sack Method.

The Potato Sack Method: A Compassionate Approach to Physical Intervention

It all started with a conversation between two parent clients who casually mentioned having to "potato sack" their son to school. The phrase struck me—a vivid, unexpected metaphor that captured the sometimes challenging reality of parenting. When they asked if this was okay, I realized we needed a nuanced, compassionate framework for understanding physical intervention.

The Potato Sack Method isn't about control. It's about safety, connection, and protection. Just as you would carefully and gently handle a fragile bag of potatoes, parents must approach physical intervention with the utmost care and intention.

Physical intervention becomes necessary in rare, critical moments when a child's safety is paramount. These are the split-second scenarios that demand immediate action: a child running into a busy street, heading to touch a hot stove, or experiencing an uncontrollable meltdown that risks self-harm. In these moments, physical intervention isn't just acceptable; it's essential.

The key is approach. When you must physically intervene, imagine you're carrying something precious and delicate. Your touch should communicate protection, not punishment. Use minimal force but maintain a firm grip. Your body language and tone should remain calm, almost reassuring. This isn't about overpowering your child but about creating a safe, contained space.

Verbal communication remains crucial. Even as you physically hold your child, speak softly and consistently. "I'm holding you because I need to keep you safe." This becomes a mantra of protection, not restriction. Your words and touch work together to communicate that this intervention comes from a place of love and care.

Emotional regulation is your most powerful tool. Children can sense tension, fear, or anger. If you approach physical intervention from a place of dysregulation, the entire experience becomes traumatic. Instead, focus on maintaining your own calm. Breathe slowly. Keep your movements deliberate and gentle. Your emotional state will help ground your child, transforming a potentially frightening experience into a moment of safety.

The Potato Sack Method is about those moments when your primary job is protection—when love looks like holding, containing, and keeping your child safe, even when they might resist.

Below are just a few scenarios where "potato sacking" is not only appropriate but essential.

Immediate Physical Danger

- ◈ Your child is running into a busy street.
- ◈ They're about to touch a hot stove.
- ◈ They're about to fall from a high surface.
- ◈ You're together in a parking lot with moving vehicles.
- ◈ They're walking near steep drops or dangerous edges.

Preventing Self-Harm

- ◈ They are having a severe meltdown and might hurt themselves.
- ◈ They are exhibiting destructive behaviors that could cause immediate injury.
- ◈ They are hitting themselves or others uncontrollably.

Crisis Management

- ◈ When a child is completely dysregulated and needs physical containment such as removing them from an overstimulating event to help them calm down in a quieter environment
- ◈ When a situation requires immediate medical or therapeutic intervention

Physical intervention is a delicate, rare necessity in parenting that should only be used as an absolute last resort, solely focused on ensuring a child's immediate safety with maximum emotional containment. The goal is always protection, implemented through gentle, deliberate actions that communicate care and safety, followed by a careful process of reconnection and understanding. These moments, while challenging, become powerful demonstrations of a parent's commitment to keeping their child safe, transforming a potentially frightening experience into an opportunity for deeper trust and connection.

In the landscape of parenting, these moments are rare. But when they occur, they become powerful demonstrations of your commitment to your child's safety and well-being. The Potato Sack Method isn't just a technique; it's a philosophy of protection, delivered with compassion.

Question: "Is it ever okay to yell at my child?"

Yelling is a primal response that reveals more about your internal state than your child's behavior.

 Remember, your thoughts directly impact how you feel. When you find yourself on the verge of yelling, it's a clear signal that you've become dysregulated—your emotional brain has taken over, hijacking your ability to connect and communicate effectively.

The PCN Method teaches that yelling is fundamentally a breakdown of perspective. It's what happens when you lose sight of your child's experience and get swept up in your own emotional tornado. As you work on developing your perspective—truly understanding your child's underlying needs and your own emotional triggers—you'll discover something remarkable: yelling becomes less and less frequent.

Think of yelling as a warning light on your parenting dashboard. It's telling you that

- ◈ you're feeling overwhelmed
- ◈ you've lost connection

- ◈ your emotional regulation needs attention
- ◈ you've stepped outside of the PCN Method's core principles

Does this mean you're a bad parent if you yell? Absolutely not. You're human. What matters is how you repair and reconnect after those moments.

If yelling happens,

1. pause and take a breath
2. recognize you've become dysregulated and may need to step away to gain perspective
3. use your nurture (*N*) strategies:

- ◈ Apologize and own your part in the problem.
- ◈ Use "try agains" to increase trust to repair and resolve the conflict in a more meaningful way.

 Remember: Each time you catch yourself before yelling, each time you stop midyell and reset, each time you apologize and reconnect—you're rewiring your own neural pathways. And every moment like this is an opportunity to come back to connection.

Question: "What if my child completely ignores me as I try these new methods?"

Ignore is the language of disconnection. When your child refuses to engage, it's not defiance; it's protection. They're telling you, through their silence, that they don't yet feel safe enough to respond. This isn't about punishing or forcing compliance but about rebuilding the bridge of trust that may have been damaged over time.

Your child has learned to protect themselves from vulnerability based on past interactions. Perhaps you've inadvertently dismissed their feelings, solved their problems too quickly, or responded with frustration when they struggled to communicate. Now they're waiting to see if this time is different.

The key is to communicate that you're making these changes because you deeply care about your relationship. Take ownership of your past missteps, acknowledging that while your previous approaches were unintentional, you now understand they weren't serving either of you.

For example:

"It seems like my words aren't landing for you right now. I want you to know that I am trying and genuinely interested in understanding what's going on with you. I promise to listen without judgment when you're ready to talk."

Or:

"I'm learning that I haven't always been the best listener. I used to jump in with solutions or get frustrated when things didn't go smoothly. I'm working on being different because our relationship matters to me, and I want to truly understand you."

Most importantly, remember that you are ultimately guiding the interaction. While you're creating space for connection, it's crucial to communicate that they have a choice—but choices come with consequences. This is the essence of self-determination.

Question: "My child is having a tantrum—what now?"

Tantrums are not battles to be won but moments of emotional flooding that require a compassionate, strategic approach. The first and most critical step is understanding that your child's brain is temporarily off-line—overwhelmed by emotions that feel bigger than their ability to manage them.

Perspective is your primary tool. Your goal is to create emotional safety before anything else. This means regulating your own emotions first, then becoming a calm, steady anchor for your child's storm. Remember, you cannot reason with a dysregulated brain.

Reflection becomes your primary intervention. Use confirming statements that validate their emotional experience: "I can see you're feeling really frustrated right now" or "This seems really overwhelming for you." These statements aren't about solving the problem but about creating a sense of being seen and understood.

For some younger children, distraction can also be a powerful strategy. Help them focus on something concrete and external—a blue square on the wall, the pattern of a carpet, or a specific shape in the room. This gentle redirection helps shift their brain from emotional chaos to a more logical state.

Remember, physical safety always takes precedence. If the tantrum involves potential harm to themselves or others, it's absolutely acceptable to use the Potato Sack Method—gently but firmly removing them from the overstimulating scenario while maintaining a calm, consistent presence.

The key is patience. Your child's brain needs to feel safe before it can return to a logical state. Your calm, consistent presence is the bridge between emotional chaos and regulation. You're not trying to stop the emotion but to provide a safe container for it to exist and then naturally subside.

Once they begin to calm, you can slowly introduce communication. "Would you like to take some deep breaths together?" or "Can you tell me what happened?" These are invitations, not demands.

Tantrums can be an opportunity to teach emotional regulation—not through words but through your own embodied example of calm, compassionate presence.

Question: What if this type of emotional language doesn't come naturally to me? I don't always know what to say."

You're not alone—many parents share this concern. The good news is that you don't have to sound like a therapist to use the PCN Method properly. You can still sound like yourself while helping your child feel seen and heard. One of the simplest and most effective ways to start is by using the Reflecting and Confirming tool you learned about in chapter 6.

Remember, Reflecting means putting into words what you see or hear from your child—like saying, "Sounds like today has been really hard," when your child says, "This is the worst day ever." You're not trying to fix the feeling or offer a solution—you're just showing you're tuned in.

While Confirming takes it a step further by checking that you're really understanding your child's experience. A simple, "Am I getting that right?" or "Does that sound like how you're feeling?" can go a long way.

Together, these small but powerful tools help you build emotional language naturally, one conversation at a time.

Special Considerations for Neurodivergent Children

Neurodivergence represents the beautiful diversity of human brain functioning, where individuals experience and process the world differently from what's typically considered "neurotypical." This includes conditions like autism, ADHD, dyslexia, and other neurological variations that shape how a child perceives, interacts with, and responds to their environment. Far from being a deficit, neurodivergence often comes with unique strengths—exceptional creativity, deep focus, innovative problem-solving, and profound empathy.

Parenting neurodivergent children requires a nuanced, deeply compassionate approach that honors their unique neurological landscape. The PCN Method remains fundamentally the same, but its implementation demands extraordinary sensitivity and individualized adaptation. Sensory experiences become critically important, with parents learning to recognize and respond to stimuli that might overwhelm or dysregulate their child in ways neurotypical children might not experience.

Visual supports become powerful communication tools, transforming abstract choices into concrete, manageable options. Where neurotypical children might understand verbal instructions, neurodivergent children often thrive with visual cues, step-by-step breakdowns, and clear, predictable frameworks. This means breaking down choices into smaller, more digestible steps, allowing extra processing time, and being prepared with specific, tangible strategies that create a sense of safety and predictability.

Seeking support is not just helpful—it's essential. Parents can connect with

- ◈ local neurodivergent support groups
- ◈ specialized occupational therapists
- ◈ neuropsychologists who understand neurodivergent experiences
- ◈ online communities of parents with similar experiences
- ◈ educational advocates who can help navigate school support systems

Emotional regulation looks different for neurodivergent children. Their experience of connection, safety, and communication might not follow typical developmental pathways. Parents become detectives of their child's unique emotional language, learning to celebrate microscopic victories and approach each interaction with profound patience and understanding. The core PCN Method principles of perspective, communication, and nurture remain unchanged—but their expression becomes a deeply personalized art of connection, requiring constant attunement, flexibility, and unconditional love.

Your child's neurodivergence is not a challenge to overcome but a unique way of experiencing the world to be understood, celebrated, and supported.

18

Congratulations – Your House of Harmony Awaits

"To those of you who have children, who are parents, I say, make sure that you listen to your children. Pay attention, because if you don't, they'll teach you something you didn't know."

—Maya Angelou

You've done something extraordinary. Through dedication, patience, and a willingness to grow, you've transformed not just your parenting approach but the very neural pathways of connection in your family.

Think back to where you started—feeling frustrated, disconnected, wondering if genuine harmony was even possible. Now you hold something powerful: a blueprint for building relationships founded on understanding, respect, and unconditional love.

The PCN Method is more than a set of techniques. It's a profound journey of transformation—for your children and for yourself. With each reflective pause, each empathetic connection, each collaborative solution, you've been literally rewiring your brain's chemistry toward harmony. Neuroscience confirms what your heart already knows: change is possible, and it begins with perspective, communication, and nurturing.

Your Remarkable Transformation

 Remember: The journey of building your House of Harmony is not about achieving a flawless, picture-perfect family dynamic. It's about persistent, compassionate growth. Each small moment of patience, each carefully considered pause before reacting, each genuine attempt to truly understand—these are the foundational bricks that transform your family's emotional landscape.

As you stand here now, you've cultivated remarkable skills that go far beyond traditional parenting techniques. You've learned to look beneath the surface of behaviors, seeing the intricate emotional needs that drive your children's actions. Where you once might have reacted with frustration, you now create safe emotional spaces that invite vulnerability and connection. Instead of controlling, you collaborate. Instead of rigidly enforcing rules, you maintain boundaries with a compassionate heart. Instead of ignoring problems, you've learned how to resolve them in meaningful, long-lasting ways.

Perhaps most importantly, you've discovered the profound art of repair. You now understand that moments of disconnection are not failures but opportunities for deeper understanding. You've learned to grow alongside your children, recognizing that parenting is a journey of mutual development—where both you and your children are constantly evolving, learning, and supporting each other.

These are not small achievements. These are fundamental transformations that will ripple through your family's relationships for generations to come. Your House of Harmony is more than a home—it's a living, breathing ecosystem of love, understanding, and mutual respect.

The Road Ahead

Challenges will inevitably arrive, casting shadows across even the most carefully constructed House of Harmony. Those moments of frustration—when tensions rise, emotions flare, and you feel yourself slipping back into old reactive patterns—are not signs of failure but a natural part of any meaningful growth journey.

But here's the profound difference: now you are equipped. The PCN Method has transformed from a set of techniques into something far deeper—a fundamental way of perceiving and responding to your family's intricate, ever-changing dynamics. It's a lens through which you view connection, a compass that guides you back to understanding when chaos threatens to take over.

When you find yourself in a "WTH" ("What the heck") moment—that instant where old triggers begin to bubble up and you can feel yourself about to react instead of respond—remember your power.

Take a breath. Just one. In that single breath, you create space. Space to step back. Space to reconnect with your foundation of perspective.

Listen. Not just with your ears but with your entire being. Listen to the emotions beneath the behavior. Listen to the unspoken needs. Listen to the vulnerability that often masquerades as defiance or withdrawal.

Connect. Reach out not with solutions but with understanding. Remind yourself and your child that you are on the same team. That you are here to understand, not to control.

Collaborate. Invite your child into the process of solving whatever challenge has emerged. Your relationship is a partnership, constantly negotiating, constantly growing.

Some days the walls of your House of Harmony will feel solid and strong. Interactions will flow with grace and ease. Conversations will feel like beautiful, intricate dances of mutual respect.

Other days it will feel messy. Chaotic. Like the foundations might crumble. Emotions will be raw. Communication will feel strained. Old patterns might briefly resurface.

Embrace it all.

These moments are not setbacks. They are feedback. Feedback that delivers opportunities to practice the skills you've cultivated. Opportunities to repair. Opportunities to demonstrate to your children that relationships aren't about perfection but about commitment, resilience, and unconditional love.

Each challenge is a chance to reinforce your House of Harmony, to make its foundations stronger, its connections more flexible, its understanding more profound.

You are not just maintaining a household. You are cultivating a living, evolving culture of connection.

A Final Invitation

You've done more than read a book—you've embarked on a transformative journey that will reshape how your family connects, communicates, and grows together. What you've built is extraordinary: not just a method but a sanctuary of genuine understanding, a home where vulnerability is welcomed and connection is the highest priority.

In the upcoming addendum, you'll find something incredibly powerful: precise scripts that bring the PCN Method to life in real-world, messy, complicated scenarios. These aren't just words on a page—they're your linguistic tool kit for navigating the most challenging parenting moments. Whether it's a tantrum at the grocery store, a homework meltdown, or a teen's emotional shutdown, having a clear road map with these scripts for these challenging moments can transform how you respond.

I encourage you to study these scripts. Practice them. Role-play them with your partner or a trusted friend. Speak them out loud until they begin to feel natural. Remember, these aren't magic words but strategic approaches that honor both your child's emotional experience and your family's need for structure.

But you don't have to walk this path alone. I'm committed to supporting you beyond these pages. Check out my website, www.DeborahWintersLCSW.com, for additional assistance:

⬧ Private coaching sessions to help you personalize the PCN Method for your unique family dynamics

⬧ Group workshops where parents learn, share, and grow together

⬧ Custom online coaching courses that include ongoing support communities where you can find connection, validation, and practical guidance

◈ Join my email newsletter for weekly parenting tips!

You've built something remarkable. Not just a house but a sanctuary of connection where every family member feels seen, heard, and loved exactly as they are. Congratulations on your House of Harmony.

The journey continues—and I'm honored to be part of it.

Addendum: PCN Method Scripts – Your Guide to Real-World Application

Welcome to the practical application section of your PCN Method journey! You've built the foundation, raised the walls, and secured the roof of your House of Harmony. Now it's time to furnish it with exactly the right tools for those challenging moments when connection feels most difficult.

What You'll Find in This Section

This addendum provides specific, age-appropriate scripts for five of the most common challenges parents are facing today (plus a bonus script):

1. Tantrums and Emotional Outbursts
2. Resistance to Chores or Responsibilities

3. Sibling Rivalry and Fighting
4. Showing Disrespect
5. Screen Time Conflicts
6. BONUS SCRIPT: Anxiety and Worries

Each scenario includes versions for older children, ages ten and older, and for younger children, ages nine and below. Depending on your child's unique personality and the specific situation at hand, you may notice some scripts are interchangeable. You'll want to adjust them based on the specific situation at hand.

When to Use These Scripts

As a reminder, the PCN Method scripts are specifically designed for those "WTH" ("What the heck") moments, when your well-intentioned attempts to help seem to create more conflict and disconnection. If your current approach is working smoothly without resistance or relationship strain, you may not need these interventions.

Signs you need the PCN Method:

1. Your attempts to help are met with increased resistance.
2. Conversations spiral into arguments.
3. Your child withdraws or becomes defensive.
4. You feel stuck in cycles of nagging and reminding.
5. Solutions that worked before suddenly stop working.
6. Your relationship feels strained by constant conflicts.

Some conversations require multiple attempts before you see change. Be patient with the process. If you start a PCN conversation and it isn't going well, it's perfectly fine to say, "I can see this isn't a good time. I may need a pause or a break to gather my perspective and try again later when I am feeling more ready."

 Remember: Each time you use these scripts, you're not just addressing an immediate challenge; you're strengthening your family's foundation of trust and understanding. I still work on my PCN Method every day!

Let's begin with your first scenario . . .

*The examples in this guide are simplified for clarity and may not encompass the full complexity of every family situation. Some children may require additional support or modified approaches due to developmental needs or mental health concerns.

SCENARIO 1: Tantrums and Emotional Outbursts

FOR TWEENS/TEENS (ten and older)

The Situation: Your thirteen-year-old just learned they didn't make the hockey team. They storm into the house, slam their bedroom door, and you can hear them crying hard. When you try to talk to them, they scream "Leave me alone!" and their emotional intensity escalates.

The *P* Phase: Pause to Gather Perspective

Resist the urge to keep attempting to help. You've already tried that, and it didn't work. You may be on your way to a full-blown WTH moment. (If they are being destructive, you always want to ensure safety first.)

Instead, pause to check in with yourself and your child. Notice your emotional thoughts: *Why are they always so dramatic when they're upset? I don't care how upset he is, we don't slam doors in this home!*

Now reframe your perspective using more logical thoughts. Remember to consider all the behavioral, emotional, and social implications you learned in chapter 4. *What does this mean to them? What does this mean for me? This must be so hard!*

Parent: "It looks like you're really upset and angry right now. I am imagining how hard this must be for you. I know how much you wanted this." (reflection)

Repeat validating and reflective observations until some de-escalation begins. If you're uncertain why your teen is upset, you can always ask what happened.

Teen: "I practiced so hard! Everyone's going to think I'm a loser!"

Resist the urge to deny their feelings and disagree. That would be a fix-it solution.

Parent: "This is a really big deal, and now it sounds like you're also worried about what others might think on top of that. I get it!"

Teen: "I'm never good enough at anything!"

Continue to resist the urge to "fix" by reminding them how "great" they are. If you feel it's important to you to compliment your child here, you can always say, "Obviously I don't believe that to be true, but I understand why you might be feeling that way right."

Look for some confirmation to know your teen feels validated.

Parent: "Am I understanding you?" (confirmation)

Continue reflecting and confirming until your teen calms down. Once your teen confirms feeling understood, you're ready to move into the communication phase.

The *C* Phase: Communicate Using Choices or Collaboration
(No consequences needed in this example.)

> Parent: "I want to support you through this. Would you prefer to talk about it, or would you like to just sit together for a while?" (choices)

Honor their choice. They may just want to vent. They may want time alone. They may want to distract themselves by doing something else. Just continue letting them know that you are there for them until they are ready.

> Parent: "What do you think will help you get through this struggle? Do you need my help coming up with ideas?" (collaboration)

Listen without fixing, and guide your teen to making decisions for themselves. They may want ideas to figure out their next steps in hockey. Or they may just want your help calming down. Whatever it is, continue to honor their feelings.

The N Phase: Follow Through with Nurture

In this example, there are many ways you can nurture your child. When they finally do calm down, you can compliment their process encouragement); let them know how hard that was but that you admire their ability to regulate. This will help your teen to identify with their coping skills and build their confidence to use this skill again in the future.

You can ask your teen if screaming like this would work in the real world and explore ways to "try again" with different coping strategies in the future.

If appropriate, make some jokes, share some hugs, and focus on something that allows for movement and exercise.

If need be, take accountability if needed: "I realize I jumped to fixing instead of listening first."

In the event there is another tryout in the future, discuss how to handle emotions and what to expect. Discuss what worked and what didn't work in this scenario.

Focus on the positive while being careful not to dismiss feelings.

FOR YOUNGER CHILDREN (under ten)
The Situation: Your six-year-old is having a complete meltdown in the grocery store because you won't buy the candy they want. They're lying on the floor screaming, kicking, and crying uncontrollably. Other shoppers are staring, and your embarrassment and frustration are rising.

Note: With young children in full meltdown, it may help to "potato sack" and remove the child from the stimuli and move to a quieter location before connecting.

The *P* Phase: Pause to Gather Perspective
Am I feeling embarrassed? Angry? Triggered? Is my child tired? Hungry? Overstimulated? Was this one "no" too many today?

> Parent: [getting down at their level] "I can see that me saying no is very disappointing to you. And that's okay." (reflection)

> Child: [crying] "But I want it! You never let me have anything!"

> Parent: "It feels so unfair when you can't have what you want, am I right?" (confirmation)

> Child: "No—you're just mean!"

Resist fix-it solutions like punishment or redirecting here.

> Parent: "You're feeling so mad at me because I said no. I get that."

Continue reflecting back on child's feelings until child begins to calm. You could also model some calm-down breaths and/or talking in a quiet voice.

The *C* Phase: Communication Using Choices or Collaboration with or without Consequences

> Parent: "It's okay for you to be upset about the candy. We are still not going to buy it today. But we can definitely make something at home using the food we already have. What do you think we should make?" (In this case, collaboration might work. If not, try a choice.)
>
> "Should we make the box of brownies or a special fruit smoothie?"

If child's temper does not persist, you can add a consequence.

[Continue to be on their level.] "I am sorry you are still so upset. You have a choice; either we make something else at home, or we leave the store and make nothing at all. Which do you choose?"

Once tempers decrease, you are ready to move into the nurture phase. Remember, you do not have to wait for your child to be "happier" to continue your shopping.

The *N* Phase: Follow Through with Nurture

You can reinforce their choice. You can highlight and positively reinforce the measures they took to calm themselves down. You can hug them and remind them how much you care for them. You can even make jokes.

Resist the urge to harp on their tantrum. If you're feeling emotional yourself, focus on the measures you took to resolve the issue and how strong you are for not rushing to "fix."

If your child using the word *mean* to describe you is not a word you want them to use, explore new words for the future when they're feeling upset.

Discuss more effective ways for them to communicate next time for the future. Even role-play if appropriate.

Set limits on behavior ahead of time the next time you enter a store together. Reflect back on what you learned from this scenario and how to handle any possible disappointment. Manage your child's expectations about what you are shopping for.

SCENARIO 2: Resistance to Chores or Responsibilities

FOR TWEENS/TEENS (ten and older)
The Situation: Your teen consistently leaves their dishes in the sink, clothes on the floor, etc. and seems resistant to helping with basic household tasks. Your reminders are met with eye rolls, excuses, or promises that never materialize.

The *P* Phase: Pause to Gather Perspective
What feels like is happening, emotional thought only: *My child is lazy. They don't appreciate me. I am so angry at them.*

Logical thought with perspective: *I am allowed to not like this behavior. I know my child is capable of doing these tasks. What might be contributing to their laziness? Are they overwhelmed with school? Struggling with their executive function? Testing independence?*

> Parent: "I notice the dishes have been piling up lately, and I'm wondering if something's making it harder to keep up with them?"

> Teen: "I'm just busy! I have so much homework and practice and everything else!"

Resist the urge to discredit their answer by saying something sarcastic like, "But you have plenty of time for your phone and friends!" This type of reaction is emotionally driven and may lead to your child shutting down immediately, aka a WTH moment.

> Parent: "Sounds like you're feeling pretty overwhelmed with all your responsibilities." (reflection)

> Teen: "Yeah, and then when I finally have free time, you want me to do chores!"

> Parent: "I hear you—it feels like chores are taking away the little free time you have. Is that right?" (confirmation)

Once teen confirms feeling understood, move into the communication phase.

The *C* Phase: Communicate Using Collaboration, Choices, and Consequences

> Parent: "I get it—you want more free time, and I want help maintaining our home. Let's put our heads together and find a solution that works for both of us."

Listen to their ideas first. If they have trouble coming up with a plan, ask them if they'd like you to come up with some solutions. If they are resistant, give them a choice either to explore solutions together or do it the way you suggested.

> Teen: "I'm thinking that we should look at my schedule and find the best nights for me to do dishes. If I

don't have practice that night, I can clean up on my own. If I have extra homework on top of practice, maybe someone can help me out."

Discuss specific details, negotiate timing, and establish clear expectations.

Parent: "I love those ideas. What do you think should happen if the tasks don't get done as agreed?"

Let them suggest consequences first.

Parent: "Those sound fair."

The *N* Phase: Follow Through with Nurture

It is extremely important to follow through with both agreements and consequences. That might sound like, "It's five p.m. on Friday, and we agreed your chores would be done before playing your video game. I see you are choosing to lose your screen time for twenty-four hours. You can try again tomorrow."

Acknowledge effort: "I noticed you loaded the dishwasher without being reminded. That really helps our household run smoothly."

Keep it light when possible: "Race you to see who can pick up their stuff faster!"

Take accountability when needed: "I realize I've been nagging instead of problem-solving with you. I'm working on that."

FOR YOUNGER CHILDREN (under ten)

The Situation: Your young child resists picking up toys or helping with other age-appropriate tasks.

The *P* Phase: Pause to Gather Perspective

Emotional thoughts: *My child is so difficult. He never does anything I ask. Why is this so hard?*

Logical thoughts: *I am allowed to be frustrated by this. I hate messes. But I also know that some kids develop faster than others. Are my expectations matching his true abilities? I also know that my child hates saying good-bye to his toys at the end of the day. He has said it makes him feel "sad."*

> Parent: "I see there are still lots of toys out even though you were asked to pick up. You cleaned up no problem last week; what's happening now?"

> Child: "It's too hard! There's too many!"

Resist the urge to dismiss their problem and go into "fix-it mode" by saying something like, "It's not that hard!"

> Parent: "All those toys feel overwhelming to pick up. It feels like such a big job." (reflection)

> Child: "Yeah! It will take forever!"

> Parent: "It feels like it would take all day to clean this up. Did I get that right?" (confirmation)

Once your child confirms feeling understood, move to the communication phase.

The *C* Phase: Communicate Using Choices or Collaboration and Consequences

> Parent: "Would you like to use the cleanup song or the timer while you tidy up?"

Let them choose.

> Parent: "And would you like to start with the blocks or the stuffed animals?"

Honor their choice.

> Parent: "Great choice! Should we make it fun by pretending we're cleanup robots or super-speedy race cars?"

Establish clear, age-appropriate expectations: "When we're done cleaning up, would you like to read a story together or play a quick game?"

If child resists, it's okay to add a choice that has a consequence: "I would really love to read a story together with you when the room is cleaned up. You have a choice to help me clean up, or I can't let you play with these toys tomorrow. And we won't have time to read."

The *N* Phase: Follow Through with Nurture

The idea is that your younger child may need something more in a situation like this than you realize. By reflecting, you stay connected. With choices, you provide control rather than telling them what to do. Now it's time to reinforce the changes together.

"I see you're choosing not to help me clean up. That makes me feel really sad because I would hate to see you lose your toys and not have time to read. Would you like a try again to avoid that from happening?"

Follow through!

If you suspect something more is going on, it's okay to return to the *P* and *C* phases to learn about their needs before setting up consequences.

Always reinforce positive behavior and celebrate effort: "You worked so hard putting all the blocks in the basket!"

SCENARIO 3: Sibling Rivalry and Fighting

FOR TWEENS/TEENS (ten and older)

The Situation: Lauren (thirteen) and Tyler (eleven) are watching TV together. Lauren is engrossed in her show when Tyler suddenly grabs the remote and changes the channel. Lauren immediately kicks Tyler, who yells, "Mom! Lauren kicked me!"

The *P* Phase: Pause to Gather Perspective

In the past, you may have used your emotions to react quickly, go into "fix-it mode," and jump to the defense of your son during a conflict like this. "How dare you hit your brother! Go to your room!" Unless it is a true safety concern, it's okay for you to step back and use your PCN Method. This will take you out of the "judge" role, which can actually lead to more sibling rivalry as your kids think you are taking sides.

Perspective check: *I am allowed to not like hearing them argue. It's a trigger for me because I just wish they could get along. But I know they're also going to get annoyed with one another whether I agree with it or not. Why would Tyler take over the TV like that? And why does Lauren think it's okay to kick? Is someone trying to gain power? Or needing attention?*

> Parent: "Hey, sounds like you guys are having a hard time. What's going on? Who would like to speak first? If you can't decide, we can flip a coin."

> Lauren: "He *always* does this! He thinks he can just take over whatever I am watching!"

> Parent: "It sounds like you're saying Tyler completely disregarded your space and what you were enjoying. Did I get that right?" (reflection and confirmation)

Lauren: "Yeah, and I bet now I'm going to get in trouble for kicking him!"

Parent: "It's definitely not okay to kick anyone. And while I can understand why Tyler frustrated you, it's important that you learn how to handle your frustrations without physically hurting someone. We can talk more about that later."

Parent to Tyler: "Help me understand what happened before you changed the channel."

Tyler: "She's been watching forever! It's not fair!"

Parent: "It sounds like you were feeling left out of the TV choice." (reflection)

Tyler: "She never lets me pick anything!"

Parent: "You're feeling like you don't get enough say in what to watch. Is that right?" (confirmation)

Once both children feel understood, bring them together for the communication phase.

The *C* Phase: Communicate Using Choices, Collaboration, and Consequences

Parent: "What I am hearing is that it may be time to learn a better system for sharing the TV so everyone is happy. I'd love to hear your ideas on what that might look like."

Listen to both children's ideas while guiding the discussion toward solutions that work for everyone. Use reflective listening and confirmation, when need be, to make sure everyone continues to feel heard and validated.

If they are having trouble coming up with their own ideas, ask them if they'd like your help. If they refuse, let them know they have two choices: to come up with their own ideas or listen to yours.

If one child is more willing to work on ideas than the other, just make sure the other is genuinely okay with the choices made.

Continue to guide and not judge! This is *their* problem to solve!

Don't forget to collaborate on the consequences.

> Parent: "What should happen if someone doesn't respect the agreements we make?"

Before wrapping on the collaboration discussion, you must discuss the importance of safety and keeping each other's hands (and feet!) to themselves. While you want your kids to create their own consequences to provide that sense of control and autonomy over the outcome of their lives, physical violence can lead to safety concerns. This is where you would add your own logical consequence for being unsafe and hitting in addition to their resolutions for sharing the TV respectfully.

> Parent: "Hitting is never acceptable. If I see you hitting again, I am taking away your social privileges for the entire week. No ifs, ands, or butts."

The *N* Phase: Follow Through with Nurture

It is very important to follow through with their agreed-upon system. If they falter, use the phrase, "I see *you* are choosing the consequence of _____. You can try again tomorrow."

If you want to give them an opportunity to try again in the moment, tell them, "That wasn't a respectful way to handle disagreement. Would you like to try again?"

Always acknowledge cooperation and add some positive reinforcement to solidify changes. And encourage them to notice their improvements too! "I notice you're both following our new TV agreement. I love seeing you guys work together. How good does it feel to get along?"

If old habits of yours crept in, take accountability: "I sometimes favor one person's side without hearing both perspectives. I'm working on that."

Note: This example assumes Tyler wasn't seriously hurt. If he was, tend to him first while letting Lauren know you'll still address the situation. Notice how Mom didn't over-emphasize the kick or label either child as "victim" or "aggressor." Like you learned with praise in Chapter 11, children tend to identify with and fulfill the roles we assign them. Instead, mom focused on modeled conflict resolution skills using the PCN Method while maintaining that physical responses aren't acceptable. This balanced approach helps both children develop healthy ways to resolve disagreements while ensuring everyone's safety.

FOR YOUNGER CHILDREN (under ten)
The Situation: Ben (eight) has been deeply focused on building with his blocks for thirty minutes. His sister, Joanie, (five) moves some of her blocks into his building area. Feeling his space invaded, Ben pushes her blocks down. Joanie bursts into tears, screaming.

The *P* Phase: Pause to Gather Perspective

In the past, your emotional reaction may have been to rush to comfort Joanie or immediately scold Ben for destroying her blocks. Unless safety is at risk, step back and use your PCN Method to avoid taking sides.

Logical perspective check: *I'm allowed to feel overwhelmed by the screaming. It triggers my urge to fix this quickly. But let me think—Ben was really focused on his project. Having his space invaded probably felt threatening. And Joanie likely just wanted to be part of what he was doing. This isn't just about blocks; it could also be about boundaries and attention. What can I teach them here about conflict resolution?*

> Parent: "I can see some big feelings happening here. Let's take a breath together and talk about what happened."

> Parent to Ben: "You were working really hard on your building. What happened when Joanie's blocks came into your space?"

> Ben: "She *always* ruins everything! I was making something special!"

> Parent: "You had been concentrating on your project for a long time, and it felt like your space was invaded. Did I get that right?" (reflection and confirmation)

> Ben: "Yeah! And now I have to start all over!"

> Parent: "It's really frustrating when someone comes into your space without asking. And while I understand why you got mad, we need to find better ways to protect your space without destroying things. We'll work on that later. Let's hear what your sister has to say."

Parent to Joanie: "Can you tell me what you were trying to do with your blocks?"

Joanie: [sniffling] "I wanted to build with Ben!"

Parent: "It looks like you really wanted to be part of Ben's building project." (reflection)

Joanie: "He never plays with me!"

Parent: "You're feeling left out and really want to play with your brother. Is that right?" (confirmation)

The *C* Phase: Communicate Using Choices and Consequences

Parent: "We need to figure out how to make building time work better for both of you. Would you like to hear some ideas?"

Offer simple choices: "We could use tape on the floor to make special building zones, take turns being the Master Builder and Assistant Builder, or make a sign that says, 'Please Ask Before Joining.'"

Make it age appropriate and fun: "Should we use Building Time Tickets to ask for joining time, or should we make special Builder Badges that show when it's okay to join?"

Discuss consequences gently: "What should happen if someone forgets to respect building space?"

Guide them toward realistic solutions: "Should blocks have a time-out, or should we practice building in separate rooms?"

The *N* Phase: Follow Through with Nurture

Follow through consistently but warmly: "I see you chose to enter building space without asking. Would you like to try again with your ticket/badge?"

Make repair opportunities clear: "Oops, we had a building space problem. Let's try again—this time using our words."

Use lots of specific praise: "Ben, I noticed you asked Joanie if she wanted to join when you were ready!" Or "Joanie, you're doing great waiting for your turn to build!"

 Remember: You are teaching your young children how to respect one another's boundaries by validating their feelings and modeling respect. In addition, the more power you give to a "bad behavior," the more that reinforces the child's need for attention. By keeping them involved in the decision, providing simple and fun choices, you are teaching them HOW to do things differently. This will increase cooperation for the long haul. What better gift to teach (aka discipline!) to your kids!

SCENARIO 4: Showing Disrespect

FOR TWEENS/TEENS (ten and older)
The Situation: You ask your fourteen-year-old daughter, Gianna, to clean her room before going out with friends. She dramatically rolls her eyes, sighs loudly, and mutters, "Whatever," in a disrespectful tone. Your immediate urge is to punish the attitude by canceling her plans.

The *P* Phase: Pause to Gather Perspective
In the past, you might have emotionally reacted to the disrespect with consequences or gotten into a power struggle. Unless there's a serious

violation of family values, step back and use your PCN Method to understand what's really happening.

Logical perspective check: *I'm allowed to feel triggered by this disrespect. It makes me want to show her she can't talk to me that way. But let me think—why such a strong reaction to a simple request? Is she feeling controlled? Overwhelmed? Is this about the room, or is something else going on? Remember: disrespect often masks other feelings, and kids her age sometimes roll their eyes or act defiant to display independence.*

> Parent: "I noticed that request seemed to hit a nerve. I'm wondering what's going on for you?"
>
> Gianna: "You're *always* telling me what to do! I was just about to clean it anyway!"
>
> Parent: "Ah, so when I made the request, it felt like I was controlling you, especially if you were already planning to do it." (reflection and confirmation)
>
> Gianna: "Yeah, and now you probably want to cancel my plans just because I had an attitude!"
>
> Parent: "I can see why you'd think that. That is typically what I would do in the past. But before thinking about consequences, I want to discuss ways we can both communicate respectfully to avoid creating more problems. Especially ones that take away your independence or require punishment.

 Remember: Respecting earns respect, not demanding it!

The *C* Phase: Communicate Using Collaboration and Consequences

> Parent: "How can we work together to figure out how
> to handle these moments better?

Let you and your teen share ideas while you guide them toward real solutions. "What would help you feel more trusted to manage your responsibilities?" "How could I check in with you in a way that feels less controlling?" "What if we created some agreements about how we talk to each other, even when we're frustrated?"

Don't forget about consequences: "What do you think should happen when either of us breaks our communication agreements?"

Let them suggest appropriate consequences: "If I nag instead of trust, or if you respond with disrespect, how should we handle that?"

The *N* Phase: Follow Through with Nurture

Following through consistently with connection is so important for the changes to stick! "I hear disrespect in your tone. Are you truly upset or just falling into old habits? I would hate to see you choose the consequence over something we can resolve appropriately. Would you like a try again to respond differently"

Make repair opportunities clear: "We both slipped into old patterns there. Want to restart this conversation?"

Take accountability when needed: "I realize I sometimes jump to controlling rather than collaborating. I'm working on that."

Use positive reinforcement: "I noticed how you calmly expressed your frustration earlier—that took real maturity." "Thank you for letting me in and for being honest with your feelings."

FOR YOUNGER CHILDREN (under ten)

The Situation: You ask your six-year-old son, Max, to put away his toys before dinner. He continues playing as if he hasn't heard you, then says, "No! I don't want to!" when you repeat the request. Your instinct is to raise your voice or threaten consequences.

The *P* Phase: Pause to Gather Perspective

In the past, your emotional frustration might have led you to use fix-it methods like trying to control the situation. But you've learned that controlling tendencies can lead to more power struggles. Unless there's an immediate safety concern, step back and use your PCN Method to understand what's happening beneath the behavior.

Logical perspective check: *I'm allowed to feel frustrated about being ignored. It triggers me when he acts like I'm not even here. But let me think—he's deeply engaged in play right now. Is this about defiance, or is he struggling with transitions? Is he feeling powerless? Overwhelmed? Remember: my kid isn't* giving *me a hard time; they are* having *a hard time.*

> Parent: [getting down at child's level] "I see you're really enjoying your game right now."
>
> Max: "I'm not done! I can't stop now!"
>
> Parent: "Ah, it feels really hard to stop in the middle of something fun." (reflection)
>
> Max: "But I'm just about to win!"
>
> Parent: "That's so exciting! I see you're worried about losing your place in the game, and that makes it hard to listen. Did I get that right?" (confirmation)

The *C* Phase: Communicate Using Choices and Consequences

> Parent: "We still need to get ready for dinner, but maybe we can find a way that feels better. Would you like some

choices? Would you like two more minutes with a timer or to save your game exactly as it is for later?"

Make it playful: "Should we clean up like race car drivers or ninja warriors?" or "Would you like to use your robot voice or superhero voice to tell your toys good night?"

Include natural consequences: "If we take too long cleaning up now, that means less time for stories before bed. Which would you prefer?"

It's okay to guide them toward understanding: "What could we do next time to make stopping easier?"

The *N* Phase: Follow Through with Nurture

Follow through consistently but with warmth: "I see you're choosing less story time by continuing to play. Would you like a try again?"

Make transitions easier: "In five minutes, it will be cleanup time. Would you like a reminder at three minutes?"

Use positive reinforcement: "Wow! You stopped playing when the timer went off!" or "I love how you found a safe spot for your toys!"

 Remember: Young children experience their world primarily through play and struggle with sudden transitions in their day. By offering them clear, simple choices and maintaining consistent responses, you create the security they need to thrive. When you transform directions into playful interactions, you're speaking their language and naturally reducing resistance. And by celebrating their moments of cooperation, you are building their internal motivation while strengthening your relationship.

SCENARIO 5: Screen Time Conflicts

The following scripts are taken directly from my Screen Time Harmony course for parents of tweens and teens. You can find this course on my website www.DeborahWintersLCSW.com. A script for younger children can be found at the end of this section below.

A Note About Screen Time:
Excessive screen time can significantly impact your child's developing brain, affecting their behavior, emotional regulation, and ability to tolerate everyday situations. The intense stimulation from screens can make it harder for children to engage in normal activities, regulate their emotions, and develop crucial social skills. While screens are part of modern life, establishing consistent, healthy boundaries helps protect your child's developing brain and supports their ability to manage transitions, regulate emotions, and engage meaningfully with the world around them.

If you are interested in gaining more comprehensive material on how to reduce your child's screen time habits in seven days using the PCN Method, check out my e-course, Screen Time Harmony at www.DeborahWintersLCSW.com.

Script #1: Setting Time Limits

The *P* Phase: Pause to Gather Perspective

> Parent: "I've noticed you've been spending a lot of time on your phone lately. Before we talk about limits, I'd like to understand what you enjoy about it. Can you tell me about your favorite apps or activities?"

Teen: "I use it to stay in touch with friends, play games, and watch videos. It helps me relax and feel connected."

The *C* Phase: Communication Using Collaboration and Consequences

Parent: "Ah, I totally get why that's important to you. I feel the same way about my phone. Being connected to friends and having downtime is definitely valuable. I just want to make sure you're able to balance phone time with other important aspects of your life. Let's work together to create a plan that allows you your phone time while ensuring you've made time for other activities. What do you think would be a fair amount of daily screen time?"

Teen: "Maybe three hours on weekdays and five hours on weekends?"

Parent: "That's a good start. How about we try two hours on weekdays and four hours on weekends—and after your other activities are take care of? We can adjust if needed. What do you think?"

Teen: "Okay, I can try that."

Parent: "Great. Now, let's discuss what happens if you go over the agreed time. What do you think would be a fair consequence?"

Teen: "Maybe losing an hour of screen time the next day?"

Parent: "That sounds reasonable. Let's also add that if you consistently stay within the limits for a month and are balancing your other activities, we can discuss increasing the time slightly. Does that work for you?"

Teen: "Sounds fair. Thank you!"

The *N* Phase: Follow Through with Nurture
A week later, the teen has gone over the time limit.

Parent: "I've noticed you've gone over your screen time limit today. This means you have chosen to have one hour less screen time tomorrow. I know it's challenging, but I believe you can manage your time better. Is there anything I can do to help you stay on track?"

Teen: "Could you remind me when I'm getting close to my limit?"

Parent: "Sure, I can do that. Let's also brainstorm some activities you enjoy that don't involve screens, so you have alternatives when your time is up."

Script #2: Device Use During Meals

The *P* Phase: Pause to Gather Perspective

Parent: "I've noticed we all tend to use our phones during meals lately. Before we talk about changing this, I'd like to understand what you get from using your device during meals. Can you share your thoughts?"

Teen: "Well, sometimes I'm in the middle of a conversation with friends, or I might get an important notification. Plus, it's just a habit now."

Parent: "I appreciate you explaining that. I can see why staying connected is important to you, and how it's become a routine. I'm wondering if we can find a way to balance that with having more engaged family time during meals."

The *C* Phase: Communicate Using Collaboration and Consequences

Parent: "Let's work together to come up with a plan for device-free meals that we all can agree on. What are your ideas?"

Teen: "Maybe we could have device-free dinners, but breakfast and lunch can be more flexible?"

Parent: "Oh, I like that. I never thought of that as a solution. How about we start with device-free dinners on weekdays and see how that goes? We can adjust if needed."

Teen: "Okay, I can try that. But what if I'm expecting an important message?"

Parent: "That's a valid concern. What do you think is a good solution?"

Teen: "How about if I am expecting something truly important, I can let you know before dinner but keep my phone on the counter, on silent? Then I can quickly check it if needed, but otherwise, it stays there."

Parent: "Done."

Parent: "Great. Now, let's discuss what happens if one of us uses a device during our agreed-upon device-free meals. What do you think would be a reasonable consequence?"

Teen: "Maybe whoever uses their device has to do the dishes that night?"

Parent: "That's a creative idea. Let's go with that. And if we all manage to stick to our agreement for a full month, we could plan a special family outing as a reward. How does that sound?"

Teen: "I like that idea."

The *N* Phase: Follow Through with Nurture
A week later, during dinner, the teen checks their phone.

Parent: "I noticed you checked your phone during dinner. Remember our agreement? This means you'll be doing the dishes tonight. I know it's a habit we're all trying to break, and it's not easy. Is there anything we can do to make it easier for you to disconnect during meals?"

Teen: "Maybe we could have some conversation starters or games to play during dinner? That might make it more interesting."

Parent: "Okay. I am not great at dinner games, so this will be new for me too. Let's brainstorm some ideas for that after you finish the dishes. I appreciate your willingness to stick to our agreement and find ways to improve our family dinners."

Script #3: Nighttime Device Usage

The *P* Phase: Pause to Gather Perspective

Parent: "I've noticed you've been using your phone quite late at night recently. Before we discuss this further, I'd like to understand what you find valuable about using your device at that time. Can you share your thoughts?"

Teen: "Well, it's when I can really relax and catch up with friends. Everyone's online then, and I don't want to miss out. Plus, I use it to wind down before sleep."

Parent: "I appreciate you explaining that. I can see why that time feels important for connecting with friends and relaxing. I'm concerned about how it might be affecting your sleep and energy levels; have you noticed that too?"

The *C* Phase: Communicate Using Collaboration and Consequences

Teen: "Sort of. I notice when I get better sleep, I get up on time and don't get as distracted in class the next day."

Parent: "Let's work together to find a balance that allows you some wind-down time but also ensures you get enough sleep. What ideas do you have?"

Teen: "Maybe I could stop using my phone an hour before bedtime instead of right up until I sleep?"

Parent: "That's a great start. How about we aim for devices off by ten on school nights and eleven on weekends? We could also look into some alternative wind-down activities that don't involve screens."

Teen: "Ten p.m. seems early. Could we try ten thirty on school nights?"

Parent: "Okay, let's start with that and see how it goes. Now, what do you think would be a fair consequence if the agreement isn't followed?"

Teen: "If I use my phone past the agreed time, maybe I have to hand it over to you an hour earlier the next night?"

Parent: "That sounds reasonable. And if you consistently stick to the agreement for a month, and you've proven to get up on time and your grades are good, we could consider extending the time by fifteen minutes. Does that work for you?"

Teen: "Yes, I can try that."

The *N* Phase: Follow Through with Nurture

A week later, the parent notices the teen using their phone at eleven on a school night.

Parent: "I see you're choosing to hand over your phone at nine thirty tomorrow night. I know it's challenging to change habits, but I believe you can do it. Have you tried any of the other relaxing activities you came up with?

Teen: "Could you maybe remind me fifteen minutes before the cutoff time?"

Parent: "I am not available to monitor your time. This responsibility is yours in order to earn trust. But I am happy to brainstorm alternatives to helping you manage your time, including other relaxing activities you could do instead of using your phone before bed. You can try again in a few days."

Script #4: Avoiding the Family for Screens

The *P* Phase: Pause to Gather Perspective

Parent: "I've noticed you've been spending a lot of time on your device when we're all together as a family. Before we discuss this further, I'd like to understand what you find engaging about using your device during these times. Can you share your thoughts?"

Teen: "Well, sometimes family time can be boring, and I have interesting things happening online. My friends are always sharing stuff, and I don't want to miss out."

Parent: "I didn't realize you felt that way. It makes it easier for me to understand now and not take things personally."

The *C* Phase: Communicate Using Collaboration and Consequences

Parent: "Let's work together to find a balance that allows you to stay connected but also gives us quality family time. What ideas do you have?"

Teen: "Maybe we could have specific family times when we all agree to put our devices away?"

Parent: "That's a great suggestion. How about we designate two evenings a week as family nights, where we all put our devices away and do something together? We could take turns choosing the activity."

Teen: "That could work. Can I suggest we keep it to just an hour or two each time?"

Parent: "Sure, let's start with that. How about Tuesday and Saturday evenings from seven to nine? Now, what do you think would be a fair consequence if someone uses their device during this time?"

Teen: "If someone uses their device, they have to plan the next family night activity?"

Parent: "I like that idea. It's a natural consequence that keeps things positive. And if we all stick to the plan for a month, maybe we could plan a special family outing as a reward. How does that sound?"

Teen: "That sounds fair. I'm willing to give it a try."

The *N* Phase: Follow Through with Nurture

Parent: "I've noticed that our family time has been interrupted by phone use lately. I'd like to discuss a new rule to help us stay more connected during these moments. What do you think about putting away our devices during all family activities?"

Teen: "That's not fair! I get important messages from friends or school and need to have my device. I promise I won't look at it anymore."

Parent: "I understand and truthfully don't want to not have any devices either. I just want to find a balance. What is a reasonable solution?"

Teen: "How about we agree to keep our phones away, but if someone feels they absolutely need to check their device, they let the family know and can do so briefly?"

Parent: "While that sounds reasonable, I know how distracting phones can be. I am willing to give it another try, but if I see it continues to be a disturbance, we'll have to go back to abstinence. I want to trust that you're capable of handling this."

Teen: "I want you to trust me. Thank you for letting me try again."

Parent: "Your input is really valuable, and I appreciate your openness to this idea."

Script #5: Avoiding Household Responsibilities

The *P* Phase: Pause to Gather Perspective

Parent: "I've noticed you've been spending a lot of time on your device when there are household tasks to be done. This makes me feel like you're taking advantage of me and just waiting for me to do your responsibilities. Is that the case?"

Teen: "Not really. I was going to get to my chores; I was just making plans and got distracted. Chores are also boring. But I don't mean to make you feel like I am taking advantage."

Parent: "I appreciate your honesty. I can see why you'd prefer engaging with interesting content rather than doing chores. But how can I trust you if I see you on your device rather than helping out?"

The *C* Phase: Communicate Using Collaboration and Consequences

Parent: "Let's work together to find a balance that allows you some screen time but also ensures household tasks get done. What ideas do you have?"

Teen: "Maybe I could do my chores first and then have screen time as a reward?"

Parent: "That's a great starting point. How about we create a daily checklist of tasks, and once they're completed, you have free time for your device? We could also set a time limit for when chores need to be done by."

Teen: "That could work. Can we keep the chore list reasonable? And maybe have some flexibility on weekends?"

Parent: "Absolutely. Let's create the list together to make sure it's fair. We can have a slightly different system for weekends. Now, what do you think would be a fair consequence if the chores aren't completed?"

Teen: "If I don't finish my chores by the agreed time, maybe I lose an hour of screen time that day?"

Parent: "That sounds reasonable. And if you consistently complete your chores for a month without reminders, we could consider adding some extra screen time as a reward. How does that sound?"

Teen: "I'm willing to give it a try."

The *N* Phase: Follow Through with Nurture

A week later, the parent notices the teen using their device before completing their chores.

Parent: "I see you're choosing to use your device before completing your chores. Remember our agreement? This means you'll have one hour less screen time today. I know it can be tempting to put off chores, but I believe you can manage your time better. Is there anything I can do to help make the chores more manageable for you?"

Teen: "Could we maybe make a playlist to listen to while doing chores? That might make it less boring."

Parent: "That's a great idea! Let's create a playlist together. And remember, you can always ask for help if a task seems overwhelming. I appreciate your willingness to stick to our agreement and find ways to make chores more enjoyable."

FOR YOUNGER CHILDREN (under ten)
The Situation: Your young child has meltdowns when screen time ends, begs for "just five more minutes," or tries to negotiate for more time.

The *P* Phase: Pause to Gather Perspective
Parent's internal check: *This daily battle is never-ending! It makes me anxious knowing the meltdown is coming. But let me think—Is their brain fried from screen time? Is the transition from something fun to something not fun super overwhelming? Is my child ready for all this screen time independence?*

Parent: "I see you're really enjoying your game right now." (reflection)

Child: "I'm almost at the next level!"

Parent: "You're excited about reaching that next level, and it feels really disappointing to stop now." (reflection)

Child: "Yeah, and it's not fair!"

Parent: "Having to stop in the middle of something fun feels really unfair, am I right?" (confirmation)

The *C* Phase: Communicate Using Choices

Parent: "I know this game is really important to you. Would you like the five-minute timer to have a silly sound, or should I give you a two-minute warning?"

Wait for child to choose.

> Parent: "And when screen time is done, would you like to have snack time or play with your blocks?"

Honor their choice.

> Parent: "Should we save your game progress now or take a quick picture of your score to remember for next time?"

If child refuses to go along with your suggestions, it's okay to implement consequences to help them understand you mean business. That might sound like, "I respect how much you love your game, and I am sorry it makes you feel upset to turn it off. Will you be shutting it down, or will I have to take it?"

It is okay for your child to be unhappy with the choices. What is most important is that you're respecting their autonomy with the right to choose. Not every choice is going to be an easy one!

The *N* Phase: Follow Through with Nurture

Whether your child cooperates quickly or not, make sure to point out how hard the decision was and how proud of them you are for making it.

> Parent: "I know that was super hard! But you turned off the tablet when the timer rang, and I am so proud of you! Now we can get started with [chosen next activity]. That took great control!"

Manage expectations for the next time: "Tomorrow, we'll use our timer again, and I'll have our next fun activity ready to go before screen time. Each time we practice, our power-down routine gets stronger! So, what will you say when I ask you to get off your screen?"

Implement a try again: "Looks like we need a try again with our power-down routine. Would you like to restart our timer and show me your calm power-down? Let's practice our transition one more time—I know you can do this! You're learning how to handle big feelings when things end. I'm right here to help you through this tricky part. You've got this—just like we practiced."

By maintaining this consistent approach—connecting before directing, offering simple choices, and following through with playful nurturing—you gradually help your child build the skills they need to handle transitions more smoothly. Over time, they learn that endings aren't permanent disasters but just transitions to the next enjoyable activity. With practice, these challenging moments become opportunities to build both skills and trust.

BONUS SCRIPT: Anxiety and Worries

A note about anxiety: Anxiety is a natural part of life that every human experiences. It's a fear response that motivates people to prepare and stay alert. For many children and teens, learning simple coping strategies through the PCN Method can help transform anxiety from a barrier into a productive force.

Remember that children often take their emotional cues from parents. Your ability to manage your own anxiety plays a crucial role in helping your child handle theirs. When parents learn to regulate their own emotional responses, they're better equipped to guide their children through anxious moments.

In some cases, individuals may need additional clinical support to manage anxiety effectively. Consider consulting a licensed mental health professional who specializes in cognitive behavioral therapy (CBT). Experts in CBT can provide personalized strategies for both parents and children, helping to build emotional resilience together. For resources, speak with your primary care provider or search for qualified therapists through professional organizations like the Association for Behavioral and Cognitive Therapies (ABCT) @ www.abct.org or Psychology Today @ www.psychologytoday.com

FOR TWEENS/TEENS (ten and older)

The Situation: Your fifteen-year-old daughter, Josie, has been invited to a party where "everyone" will be attending. She's spiraling with anxiety, checking social media obsessively to see who's going, changing her mind every few minutes about attending, and making excuses about why she can't go. You notice her becoming increasingly withdrawn and agitated as the date approaches.

The *P* Phase: Pause to Gather Perspective

Parent's emotional internal check: *I hate how anxious she is. Why does she make this so hard on herself? She needs to get a hold of herself and stop obsessing!*

Logical perspective check: *I remember what a struggle this was for me when I was her age. Knowing what I know about anxiety and fear, I have to remember that this isn't just about a party. It's about feeling socially unsafe and uncertain, which is totally natural! My job isn't to solve this but to help her navigate it.*

> Parent: "I notice you seem pretty stressed about Saturday's party. Want to talk about it?"
>
> Josie: "I just don't feel like going anymore. It's probably going to be lame anyway."

Resist the urge to go into "fix-it mode" by trying to convince her that it will different.

> Parent: "I hear you trying to convince yourself it's not worth going, but I'm wondering if there's more to it?" (reflection)

> Josie: "Everyone else already knows each other so well. They all hung out all summer while I was at Grandma's. I'll probably just stand there like an idiot."

> Parent: "You're worried about feeling like an outsider, especially since others have had more time to connect. And that feels really vulnerable. Did I understand that correctly?" (confirmation)

> Josie: "Yes!"

The *C* Phase: Communicate Using Choices and Collaboration

> Parent: "I understand this feels really overwhelming. Would you be open to exploring this together—not to force any decisions but just to sort through your thoughts?"

Listen to their perspective first.

> Josie: "I want to go, but what if no one talks to me? What if I say something stupid?"

Resist the urge to say something dismissive like, "Why would no one talk to you? You're so smart, you're not stupid!" or "Everyone loves you; they should be happy to talk to you." These are "fix-it" responses.

Parent: "Those are real concerns. Would it help to break this down into smaller pieces we can look at together?"

Guide collaborative problem-solving with questions such as, "Do you really believe no one will talk to you? What does saying something 'stupid' even sound like? What if someone said that to you; would you not want to be their friend or laugh?"

Parent: "What would make you feel more comfortable about going? We can brainstorm some ideas, and you can tell me what feels manageable. Would it be helpful to have a plan B?"

Develop strategies together, but always try to let them lead with solutions first unless they ask for ideas. This helps to keep them feeling in control over the outcome, including asking you for help.

The *N* Phase: Follow Through with Nurture

Come up with a plan to make sure they know you'll follow through. That might sound like, "Whatever you decide about the party, I'm here to support you. I'll have my ringer on all night!"

Continue to use validating phrases, and avoid dismissive "fix-it" ones. "Social situations can feel really overwhelming. So many of us can relate to that! You can be anxious *and* brave at the same time."

Encourage their decision-processing skills. "I can see you're pushing through your comfort zone—that takes real courage. You're building social muscles, even if it doesn't feel like it right now."

 Remember: This collaborative and connecting strategy focuses on building their confidence in handling social situations rather than trying to eliminate their anxiety completely. Helping

them identify their own coping strategies will help them develop resilience for the future.

FOR YOUNGER CHILDREN (under 10)
The Situation: Your eight-year-old is expressing intense worry about an upcoming school presentation. They're pacing, complaining of stomachaches, and beginning to cry, saying, "I can't do it!"

The *P* Phase: Pause to Gather Perspective
Parent's emotional internal check: *He is totally lying to get out of this! I am so worried he will never know the meaning of a good work ethic. He's always looking for excuses. Someone has to teach him!*

Logical perspective check: *It's natural for someone to feel nervous about a presentation. This is important to him, and I get it. But seeing him distressed makes me feel anxious. I'm feeling anxious seeing my child so distressed. It triggers my urge to fix this or let him avoid it altogether. I have to remember that this isn't about the presentation; it's about feeling unsafe and uncertain. My job isn't to eliminate his anxiety but to help him learn to manage it.*

> Parent: "I see these worry feelings are feeling really big right now."
>
> Child: "My tummy hurts! I can't do the presentation!"
>
> Parent: "Your worry is so big it's making your whole body feel scared." (reflection)
>
> Child: "What if I mess up? What if I forget everything?"

> Parent: "You're worried about forgetting your words and having people judge you. Those thoughts feel really scary right now. Did I get that right?" (confirmation)

If the child says no, continue reflecting until they feel understood completely. Then you're ready to move on to the *C* phase.

The *C* Phase: Communicate Using Choices and Collaboration
Parent: "When our worries get this big, it helps to have some tools ready. Would you like to learn some worry-fighting strategies together?"

Offer age-appropriate choices.

> Parent: "Should we try some dragon breaths to calm our body, or would you like to draw what your worry looks like?"

Wait for child to choose.

> Parent: "And would you like to practice your presentation with your stuffed animals first, or should we start with just one person listening?"

Create a concrete plan together. (collaboration)

> Parent: "Let's make a worry plan. What would help you feel braver tomorrow?"

Guide them toward realistic strategies while honoring their ideas.

> Parent: "Should we pack a special brave stone in your pocket, or would you like to wear your lucky socks?"

The *N* Phase: Follow Through with Nurture
Manage expectations because, remember, humans like knowing what to expect. Parent might say, "I see your brave choices. Let's practice

our tools when the worries feel smaller, so they're easier to use when worries get big."

If worry doesn't disappear, continue to validate and offer choices when appropriate. "Those worry feelings are coming back. Would you like to try one of our tools?" You could also use a try again here: "Our first strategy didn't feel quite right. Should we try a different one?" or "Worries can take practice to handle. Want to try another way?"

Use positive reinforcement to solidify coping mechanisms: "You used your dragon breaths when you felt worried—that took courage!" or "You faced something scary and got through it!" or "Your brave muscles are getting stronger every time you try!"

The goal is never to eliminate anxiety—as it's there to protect us; it's part of a human's DNA—but to find ways to help your child build confidence in managing it. Stay consistent with practicing coping strategies during calmer moments so they're easier to access during stressful times. Always validate your child's feelings before moving to solutions, and celebrate every small step toward facing their fears. By maintaining connection through the process, you help your child learn that while anxiety is uncomfortable, it's manageable and they're not alone in handling it.

Final Thoughts

The PCN Method is never about perfect parenting; it's always about finding ways to communicate more effectively with intentional connection to avoid yelling, nagging, or conflict. There will be days when you nail it and days when you struggle. What matters is your commitment to understanding, connecting with, and guiding your child through life's challenges.

Addendum: PCN Method Scripts

Keep these scripts handy, but don't feel bound by them. Let them be your guide as you develop your own authentic way of using the PCN Method. With practice, these patterns will become more natural, creating lasting positive changes in your family dynamics.

 Remember: Every time you choose connection over control, understanding over argument, and nurture over negativity, you're building another brick in your House of Harmony. Keep building, keep growing, and keep connecting—one moment at a time.

References

Ainsworth, Mary D. S., Mary C. Blehar, Everett Waters, and Sally Wall. (1978). *Patterns of Attachment: A Psychological Study of the Strange Situation*. Lawrence Erlbaum.

Baumrind, Diana. (1967). "Child Care Practices Anteceding Three Patterns of Preschool Behavior." *Genetic Psychology Monographs*, 75(1), 43–88.

Beck, Aaron T. (1963). "Thinking and Depression: 1. Idiosyncratic Content and Cognitive Distortions." *Archives of General Psychiatry*, 9(4), 324–33.

Cano, Tomás, Francisco Perales, and Janeen Baxter. (2018). A Matter of Time: Father Involvement and Child Cognitive Outcomes. *Journal of Marriage and Family*, 81(1), 164–84. https://doi.org/10.1111/jomf.12532.

Denham, Susan A. (2007). Dealing with Feelings: How Children Negotiate the Worlds of Emotions and Social Relationships. *Cognition and Emotion*, 21(1), 92123. https://psycnet.apa.org/record/2007-05198-001.

Deci, Edward L., and Richard M. Ryan. (1985). *Intrinsic Motivation and Self-Determination in Human Behavior*. Springer Science and Business Media.

Doidge, Norman. (2007). *The Brain That Changes Itself: Stories of Personal Triumph from the Frontiers of Brain Science*. Viking.

References

Dreikurs, Rudolf, and Vicki Soltz. (1964). *Children: The Challenge.* Hawthorn Books.

Dweck, Carol S. (2006). *Mindset: The New Psychology of Success.* Random House.

Field, Tiffany. (2001). *Touch.* MIT Press.

Glasser, Howard. (2002). *Transforming the Difficult Child: The Nurtured Heart Approach.* Children's Success Press.

Greene, Ross W. (1998). *The Explosive Child: A New Approach for Understanding and Parenting Easily Frustrated, Chronically Inflexible Children.* HarperCollins.

Green, Susan, and Brenda L. Baker. (2011). "Parents' Emotion Expression as a Predictor of Child's Social Competence: Children with or without Intellectual Disability." *Journal of Intellectual Disability Research*, 55(4), 324–38.

Gottman, John M. (1997). *Raising an Emotionally Intelligent Child: The Heart of Parenting.* Simon & Schuster.

Gottman, John M. (1999). *The Seven Principles for Making Marriage Work.* Three Rivers Press.

Harper, Douglas. (n.d.). "Discipline." *Online Etymology Dictionary.* Retrieved February 4, 2025, from https://www.etymonline.com/word/discipline#etymonline_v_11385.

Kranowitz, Carol Stock. (1998). *The Out-of-Sync Child: Recognizing and Coping with Sensory Processing Disorder.* Perigee Books.

Lally, Philippa, C. H. M. Van Jaarsveld, Heather W. W. Potts, and Jane Wardle. (2009). "How Are Habits Formed: Modelling Habit Formation in the Real World." *European Journal of Social Psychology*, 40(6), 998–1009. https://doi.org/10.1002/ejsp.674.

Maccoby, Eleanor E., and John A. Martin. (1983). "Socialization in the Context of the Family: Parent-Child Interaction." In P. H. Mussen (Ed.), *Handbook of Child Psychology* (4), 1–101. Wiley.

Milkie, Melissa A., Kei M. Nomaguchi, and Kathleen E. Denny. (2015). Does the Amount of Time Mothers Spend with Children or

References

Adolescents Matter? *Journal of Marriage and Family*, 77(2), 355–72. https://doi.org/10.1111/jomf.12170.

Oostenbroek, J., and A. Vaish. (2019). The Emergence of Forgiveness in Young Children. *Child Development*, *90*(6), 1979–92. https://doi.org/10.1111/cdev.13069.

Perry, Bruce D., and Maia Szalavitz. (2006). *The Boy Who Was Raised as a Dog: And Other Stories from a Child Psychiatrist's Notebook*. Basic Books.

Porges, Stephen W. (2011). *The Polyvagal Theory: Neurophysiological Foundations of Emotions, Attachment, Communication, and Self-Regulation*. W. W. Norton & Company.

Provine, Robert R. (2000). *Laughter: A Scientific Investigation*. Viking.

Ryan, Richard M., and Edward L. Deci. (2000). Self-Determination Theory and the Facilitation of Intrinsic Motivation, Social Development, and Well-Being. *American Psychologist*, 55(1), 68–78. https://doi.org/10.1037/0003-066X.55.1.68.

Seligman, Martin E. P. (1998). *Learned Optimism: How to Change Your Mind and Your Life*. Pocket Books.

Siegel, Daniel J., and Tina Payne Bryson. (2011). *The Whole-Brain Child: 12 Revolutionary Strategies to Nurture Your Child's Developing Mind*. Delacorte Press.

Siegel, Daniel J., and Mary Hartzell. (2004). *Parenting from the Inside Out: How a Deeper Self-Understanding Can Help You Raise Children Who Thrive*. TarcherPerigee.

Webster-Stratton, Carolyn, and M. J. Reid. (2004). "Strengthening Social and Emotional Competence in Young Children: The Foundation for Early School Readiness and Success." *Infants and Young Children*, 17(2), 96–113. https://doi.org/10.1097/00001163-200404000-00002.

Volkow, Nora D., Gene-Juan Wang, and Joanna S. Fowler. (2011). "Dopamine in Drug Abuse and Addiction: Results from Imaging Studies and Treatment Implications." *Neuropsychopharmacology*, 36(1), 104–14.

About the Author

DEBORAH WINTERS is a licensed clinical therapist and parent coach dedicated to helping individuals and families create lasting change. With over a decade of experience, she specializes in guiding parents through conflict, strengthening family connections, and supporting teens and adults struggling with anxiety, self-doubt, and relationship challenges.

Deborah is the creator of the PCN Method, a science-backed communication framework designed to reduce conflict and foster cooperation without power struggles. She holds a post-master's in parent education and is a certified STEP (Systematic Training in Effective Parenting) leader.

As both a therapist and a mother, Deborah understands the challenges of parenting firsthand. Her compassionate, practical approach empowers families to move beyond frustration and disconnection, creating more peace, respect, and understanding at home. In addition to providing private therapy for New York residents, she offers parent coaching, workshops, and speaking engagements to help families and professionals create their own *House of Harmony*™ using the PCN Method.

www.ingramcontent.com/pod-product-compliance
Lightning Source LLC
Chambersburg PA
CBHW021712120626
46545CB00004B/1525

* 9 7 8 1 9 6 4 2 5 1 5 8 5 *